T0136355

SECRETS OF THE ANIMATOR

First Edition published 2023
by CRC Press
6000 Broken Sound Parkway NW, Suite 300, Boca Raton, FL 33487-2742

and by CRC Press
2 Park Square, Milton Park, Abingdon, Oxon, OX14 4RN

© 2023 Editions Pyramyd

Technical Proofreader: Christophe Peladan

Illustrations: Julia Peguet, except p. 15, 75, 82–83, 88, 90, 102, 105, 141, 143: Julianna Cox

CRC Press is an imprint of Taylor & Francis Group, LLC

Reasonable efforts have been made to publish reliable data and information, but the author and publisher cannot assume responsibility for the validity of all materials or the consequences of their use. The authors and publishers have attempted to trace the copyright holders of all material reproduced in this publication and apologize to copyright holders if permission to publish in this form has not been obtained. If any copyright material has not been acknowledged please write and let us know so we may rectify in any future reprint.

Except as permitted under U.S. Copyright Law, no part of this book may be reprinted, reproduced, transmitted, or utilized in any form by any electronic, mechanical, or other means, now known or hereafter invented, including photocopying, microfilming, and recording, or in any information storage or retrieval system, without written permission from the publishers.

For permission to photocopy or use material electronically from this work, access www.copyright.com or contact the Copyright Clear-ance Center, Inc. (CCC), 222 Rosewood Drive, Danvers, MA 01923, 978-750-8400. For works that are not available on CCC please contact mpkbookspermissions@tandf.co.uk

Trademark notice: Product or corporate names may be trademarks or registered trademarks and are used only for identification and explanation without intent to infringe.

ISBN: 978-1-032-11929-8 (hbk)
ISBN: 978-0-367-25200-7 (pbk)
ISBN: 978-0-429-33060-5 (ebk)

DOI: 10.1201/9780429330605

Publisher's note: This book has been prepared from camera-ready copy provided by the authors.

SECRETS OF THE ANIMATOR

Julia Peguet

CRC Press
Taylor & Francis Group
Boca Raton London New York

CRC Press is an imprint of the
Taylor & Francis Group, an **informa** business

CONTENTS

Share your creations
on social media with
#SECRETSOFTHEANIMATOR

Animation is a technique that is still somewhat misunderstood by the general public, and at times it can be quite difficult to define. Here is the definition I propose in this book: any element that moves or comes to life on screen that does not have a life of its own in real life is animated by an animator.

And you are the animator.

At an average of 4 seconds of animation per day, acquiring experience and learning from one's efforts, mistakes and successes can be a rather long learning process for an aspiring animator. This book is a compilation of knowledge, tricks and tips I've gleaned and discovered throughout my career that will help you achieve your goal of making quality animations.

What exactly are we talking about when we talk about animation?

We may come across some false friends on screen, such as motion capture, where the characters are essentially actors in costume (here, the costumes are computer generated), and rotoscoping, which is a type of graphic processing used on video images. These two techniques are mistakenly perceived as animation techniques, however in both cases they consist of filming humans in real life.

On the other hand, to further muddy the waters, pixilation, which uses human actors (i.e. objects that move of their own volition in real life), is animation because we manipulate the actors like puppets, as if they were devoid of life.

Animation relies on a basic optical principle known as persistence of vision. The eye retains the image received for a fraction of a second before "storing" it as a single image. If we show a sequence of images (with only slight changes among them) for these short fractions of a second, the brain will perceive this sequence of images as one fluid, continuous motion. Animation relies entirely on this principle: individual images are projected at constant speed of 24 images per second to create the illusion of movement.

The physical principle that animation relies upon is also the principle that led to the invention of film-making in the late 19th century. Prior to this, moving images were produced using toys such as the zoetrope (1834) or the flip book (1868), and, later, using experimental objects such as Émile Reynaud's Théâtre Optique (Optical Theater) (1888). At that time, it was easier to paint separate images by hand (i.e. animation) to depict a scene in motion than to invent a way of filming a real-life scene (motion pictures or live-action films).

Nevertheless, certain inventors made essential contributions on the way toward motion picture making, most notably Eadweard Muybridge with his studies on human and animal motion (1877-1878). He photographed these motions in archaic versions of what would become motion pictures a decade later. Even today, Muybridge is still a well-known figure in the world of animation thanks to this particular subject. For its part, at the turn of the 20th century, animation was already evolving into its own particular technique and art form, with small fictional films such as Émile Cohl's *Fantasmagorie,* the first official animated drawing (1908). However, it also became a preferred technique for creating a multitude of special effects in the burgeoning film industry, as demonstrated so remarkably by Georges Méliès (1900s) and Ray Harryhausen (1950-1960).

From Walt Disney's *Snow White*, the first full-length animated motion picture in history (1937), to the many computer animated films produced by big studios each year, not to mention famous short films such as Nick Park's *The Wrong Trousers* (1993), global hit series such as *My Little Pony* (Sunbow Productions and Marvel Productions), and independent films such as Adam Elliot's *Mary and Max* (2009), animation comes in so many different forms that it seems almost inconceivable that animators on such diverse productions would have anything in common. Yet, an animator's terrain, their specialty, their particular skill, is to recreate motion. An animator's tools, whatever form they come in, are the image, time and space.

This book is intended for the animator who creates images with intention of portraying motion, personality, emotions – simply put, life – where there was only inanimate objects before.

In animation, there are two main production methods: key-frame animation (traditional cartoons, CGI, and any other computer-assisted animations) and straight-ahead animation (all animations made directly in front of a camera – stop motion, traditional cutout animation, rostrum camera animation, sand, paint-on-glass, etc.). By default, this book is geared toward straight-ahead animation, since I, myself, am a product of the straight-ahead technique; however, most of the advice about animation in general (energy sources, timing, the actor's role, etc.) is valid for any technique.

When the advice given only concerns stop motion animation, the paragraph will be marked with white lines (see below).

The first chapter of this book will examine the fundamental principles of animation. Next, we will explore, analyze and break down the mechanics of motion, frame by frame, in chapter 2. In chapter 3, we will make some simple workable puppets for stop motion, and we will see how to recreate visual effects that will transport viewers into an artificial reality. Chapters 4 and 5 will be dedicated to an in-depth analysis of acting, which is essential to conveying a clear message and creating an emotional connection with the viewer immediately. We will examine this critical part of the animator's job in great detail for both human (chapter 4) and non-human (chapter 5) characters. In the appendices, we will take a look at different tips related to the animator's work environment and the dialogue that is established directly with the viewer.

In animation, just as in any other art form, the artist must learn and master the techniques and mechanics to be able to break the rules and find their own style. I hope this book will help you not only think about your animations but also the many tools at your disposal, and I hope it will help you take the viewer on a journey into your universe.

How to use this book

This book is intended for all animators, but certain passages are specifically written with stop motion animators in mind. A long white line (on the left) marks these passages (they may be a phrase, a paragraph, a box or even a whole section). Keep you eyes peeled!

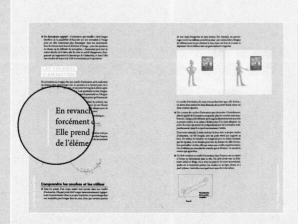
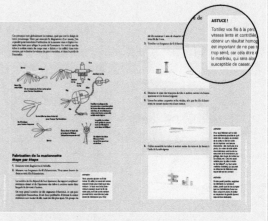

FUNDAMENTAL
PRINCIPLES
OF ANIMATION

Animation relies on the basic optical principle known as persistence of vision and on watching a sequence of images to recreate motion. Here, we will explain how these images must be made. We will look at the primary tool animators have at their disposal to calibrate their manipulations from one frame to another so that they can be read smoothly by the viewer. This tool, the cornerstone of animation, is known as the animation curve.

Straight-ahead animation versus key-frame animation

Straight-ahead animation requires the animator to move animated elements frame by frame in chronological order, starting with image 1, then 2, then 3, etc. up to the very last frame, no matter if the shot consists of 22 images or 854! Understanding a straight-ahead animation, without going through testing phases to determine the key poses in advance, presents a challenge that makes animation directly in front of a camera unique, risky and fascinating. For example, one must visualize both the direction of the motion (its curve) and the timing in order to start with the right space between image 1 and image 2. This type of animation is also risky because the slightest mistake means you will have to go back to that frame, even if it's at the very beginning, reposition elements and delete any subsequent frames in order to completely redo them. This means that you not only have to go back to the defective element but also the other characters that appear in the image which were working just fine.

In straight-ahead animation, if the mistake is here in image 3, all the subsequent images have to be redone.

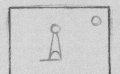

For its part, key-frame animation requires us to first put down the images that influence the direction of the motion. In other words, as soon as the direction of an element changes, we have a new key frame. Next, we establish the time an element takes to move from one pose (first key frame) to another (second key frame), for example five images. Lastly, we put the intermediate frames, known as inbetweens, between the key frames (in this case three inbetweens between the key frame in image 1 and the key frame in image 5). These inbetweens complete the element's motion fluidly from the first key frame to the second. If we just film key frames without inbetweens and instead include a freeze frame in lieu of the missing inbetweens, we will get a pretty good idea of what the animation will look like and how good it is.

Here, the key frames are images 1, 5 and 7. The inbetweens are images 2, 3, 4 and 6. If a mistake finds its way into image 3, we just redo images 2, 3 and 4.
If there is a mistake in image 6, we just redo 6. If a mistake pops up in image 5 (key frame), we redo all the associated inbetweens, in other words images 2, 3, 4 and 6, in addition to image 5 itself.

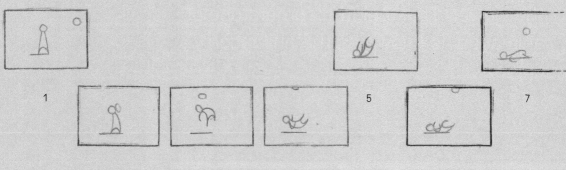

1   2   3   4   5   6   7

How Many Frames Per Second?

In traditional animation (done by hand, as opposed to computer-assisted animation and computer generated imagery), we have the choice of animating 24 frames per second (24 fps) or 12 frames per second (12 fps). Persistence of vision is best at 24 fps, but it still works at 12 fps. With less frames per second, we lose the effect of fluid, continuous motion. The viewer may begin to see a sequence of distinct images. What are the advantages and disadvantages of each speed?

✕ Some directors or studios, such as Laika (*Coraline*), prefer to work with an optimal persistence of vision and, therefore, require their animators to film each 24 frames of every second. In other words, the animators must pose the characters 24 times for one second of motion or divide each second of motion into 24 poses. The result is very realistic, but costly, since it requires twice as much animation for the same number of seconds as the second method.

✕ Other studios, like Aardman (*Chicken Run*), prefer to opt for animation at 12 fps. Each pose is photographed twice and, thus, viewed by the eye two times in a row; nevertheless, it is replaced on the retina just quickly enough by the following pose for the motion to appear fluid and continuous. The effect is imperceptible to the viewer, even though subconsciously they perceive a certain "handmade" style. This is a purposeful choice that this studio makes. A major advantage with animation at 12 fps: the animation takes less time, since there are only 12 poses per second, reducing production costs.

When an animator works on a production requiring two images per pose (12 fps), there is a possibility, at certain strategic moments, to switch to one image per pose (24 fps). There are three scenarios where making this switch is essential.

✕ **Camera movement** – Camera movements (traveling, zoom, panning) are always animated "one pose per frame" (one frame = one pose, i.e. 24 fps). Conversely, if the character in motion in front of the camera is animated "on twos" (one pose over two frames, or 12 fps), what we get is a "staircase"(or strobe) effect: the character moves while the camera is in motion, then rests in the following frame while the camera remains in motion, then moves again while the camera is in motion, before resting once again, and so on and so forth. This staircase effect is extremely uncomfortable to the eye; the shot has to be redone and the character needs to be animated at one pose per frame, at the same rate as the camera.

✕ **A speed too fast for the eye to perceive the trajectory**– Sometimes, when animating on twos, an element has such a fast trajectory, and poses (intervals) spaced so far apart from each other, that the eye is unable to connect them and perceive fluid, continuous motion. In this scenario, it is necessary to animate with one pose per frame in order to provide the eye with more information and perception points.

✕ **An enhanced dynamism** – An animator working on twos benefits from the ability to switch to one pose per frame and, thus, create a dynamic contrast in movement. Without necessarily needing to animate at one pose per frame – due to speed or perception issues –, the animator can still decide to do so in order to create a subtle change, a change that will make the animation more dynamic, which will be perceived by the viewer subconsciously.

ANIMATION CURVES

In key-frame animation, an animation curve is the interpretation of the timing between two key frames. The first and last point on the line are the key frames, and the points along the line represent all the inbetweens. Their proximity to, or distance from, one another reflects the proximity to, or distance from, the pose in question with regard to the two poses surrounding it.

In straight-ahead animation (the default perspective in this book), an animation curve is a representation in space (and on screen) not only of the spacing (i.e. the timing) between each pose of the animated object, but also its arc, its direction.

An animation curve looks like this in the two techniques:

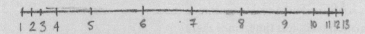

On the other hand, in straight-ahead animation, the animation curve isn't necessarily straight, since it also represents an arc in space. Thus, it adopts the physical direction of the animated object's trajectory.

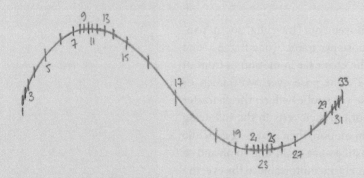

Understanding Curves and Using Them

✕ All the points of an animated body are recorded in an animation curve. Each point must move harmoniously, logically and precisely according to its specific trajectory. The character as a whole may move in one direction, while certain parts of its body move in the opposite direction. For example, a character gestures to a picture on the wall: the character's whole body moves away from the picture so as to not get in the way, but their arm and hand gesture to the picture, inviting the viewer to look.

The body's animation curve is not the same as the arm's, and, therefore, we must use two separate curves to animate them fluidly.

✗ There are as many animation curves as needed. Generally, the higher quality the animation, the more curves you have. Each little element moving separately has its own curve, even if it's part of another element. A point on a body that moves separately is worked on separately, until the movement stops.

In our example, the hand at the end of the arm will have its own curve, since its movement will be slightly delayed compared to the arm. Similarly, the hips will not move at the same times as the shoulders, and we may choose to add a rotating effect to the head, which will create an additional curve. And we can't forget about raising the eyebrows or adding a smile, either.

✗ We must visualize its animation curve in space, with a reference point on the screen or directly in our head. We must know in which direction the animated element is moving, where point B of our motion is and what the exact path is (on a curve or a straight line, and at what pace, in other words what the spacing between the intermediate frames is).

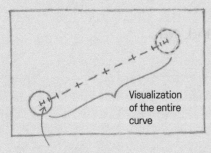

Visualization of the entire curve

Pose 2

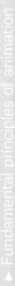

Pose 2 is critical. The first frame is the initial pose, and the second determines the trajectory. We must imagine the rest of the virtual trajectory we've just created; it must point in the right direction, like an arrow aimed at a target. To a lesser degree, it also determines the pacing (we are moving with intervals very close together as the motion starts, this pacing can therefore be set in subsequent poses). After that, just like an arrow that has been loosed, it completes its trajectory. We cannot change the direction halfway through because the viewer will perceive it as a mistake, as something unnatural. This would create a "hitch" that would force the animator to erase the frames and go back and redo the movement.

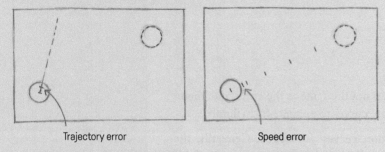

Trajectory error   Speed error

Once we have our second image, whether we complete the path or have to start over, we never, ever change the animation curve along the way. It is impossible to produce sawtooth animation curves that change every two, four or six frames.

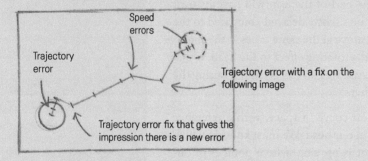

X It is important to look at the preceding frames to check the curve's continuity. If we only look at the previous frame without looking back further, we will have no idea what direction the curve is moving in or the timing between the two poses.

Personally, to determine each new pose, I continually go back over the five preceding frames.

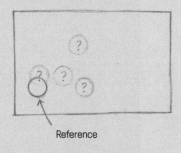

Reference

The ball can be anywhere.

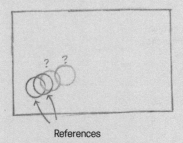

References

We now know the ball's trajectory. On the other hand, it can be accelerating or moving at a constant speed.

References

We know both the trajectory and the speed; we can place the next image with complete confidence.

A hitch (a mistake) in the animation curve makes our character look less alive. The illusion of life is lost, and the disappointed viewer, becomes aware of the technique used.

✕ An animation curve consists of a direction (shape) and intervals.

— The shape of the curve is a marker of space: it indicates the direction of the movement.

— The distance (or interval) between the poses is a marker of time: it indicates the movement's speed.

By combining these two elements (direction and speed), we will be able to pose our intervals in the right points on the screen, which will allow us to draw an accurate curve and give the animated element the right speed.

Let's look at them close up.

Direction

The animation curve isn't just about movement in space, it's also about the object's own shape and its positioning. Too often, when getting started, we think an animation curve is only an indicator of movement in space. But there's an animation curve anytime we have motion of any kind. This motion is often a movement from one point to another, but it can also have to do with the object's positioning (rotation, shift, etc.) or its shape (a complete metamorphosis, for example). The animation curve may even be a matter of varying intensity, such as the light from a fire, which will vary manually, frame by frame.

PAY ATTENTION TO THE SHADOW!

A perfect animation on screen can be betrayed by a shadow that is not animated with a perfect curve, a shadow that, either wholly or partially, jumps back and forth while the character's body looks perfect on screen.

Straight trajectory, acceleration, constant speed, then slow down

Curved trajectory, acceleration, constant speed, then slow down

S-shaped trajectory, with occasional decelerations

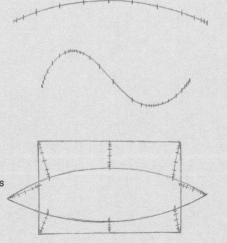

Total shape transformation with multiple animation curves on the shape's main points

Full motion with multiple animation curves on the character's main body elements

EXERCISE

Draw the animation curves between poses A and B.

▶ A bowling ball falls and rolls.

▶ A car stops at a red light.

▶ A star changes into a circle.

See the solutions at the end of the book.

Speed

In animation, space has a direct impact on time. Greater or lesser spacing between frames results in a faster or slower speed. The greater the spacing between the two poses, the faster the speed.

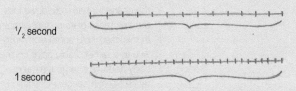

1/2 second

1 second

TIP!

When in doubt about the animation speed

It is easier on the eye to remove the second image of each pose (going from two images per pose to one image per pose) rather than adding a second image (going from one image per pose to two images per pose). It is therefore preferable to animate with two images right from the start.

On the other hand, for a rapid motion across the screen (for example, a tennis ball coming from off screen on the left to hitting an obstacle on the right side of the screen), we are almost guaranteed a strobing/blinking effect if we do not animate with one pose per frame (24 fps, or one frame per pose).

We can, thus, ask ourselves how to animate a motion more slowly after noticing that the initial spacing was too generous (i.e. the initial speed was too fast). Do we need to shoot three or more frames for the same pose, and three or more again for the following pose? If we use more than two frames for the same pose, the persistence of vision and the perception of fluid, continuous motion will be lost. We must, therefore, create more intermediate frames. For a speed that is too fast:

Persistence of vision is perfect, but motion is too fast with only ten frames.

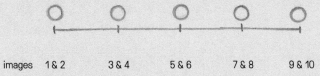

images   1 & 2   3 & 4   5 & 6   7 & 8   9 & 10

We do not want this:

Motion at a good speed (20 frames for the same distance),
but persistence of vision is lost, since we have more than two frames per pose.

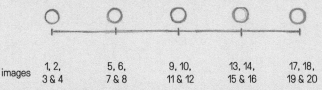

images   1, 2,   5, 6,   9, 10,   13, 14,   17, 18,
          3 & 4   7 & 8   11 & 12   15 & 16   19 & 20

But we do want this:

Motion at good speed and perfect persistence of vision,
since we have more poses, each of them lasting two frames.

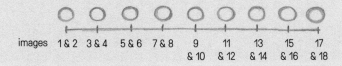

images   1 & 2 3 & 4 5 & 6 7 & 8   9   11   13   15   17
                                      & 10   & 12   & 14   & 16   & 18

By the same logic, must we create less frames to slow down and stop a swaying movement? No, a swaying movement up to a complete stop consists of the same number of inbetweens each time; the spacing simply gets smaller and smaller.

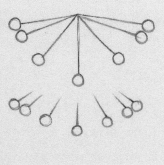

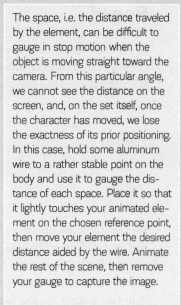

The space, i.e. the distance traveled by the element, can be difficult to gauge in stop motion when the object is moving straight toward the camera. From this particular angle, we cannot see the distance on the screen, and, on the set itself, once the character has moved, we lose the exactness of its prior positioning. In this case, hold some aluminum wire to a rather stable point on the body and use it to gauge the distance of each space. Place it so that it lightly touches your animated element on the chosen reference point, then move your element the desired distance aided by the wire. Animate the rest of the scene, then remove your gauge to capture the image.

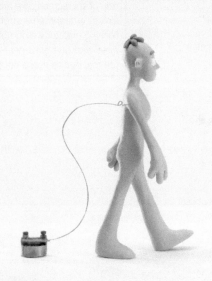

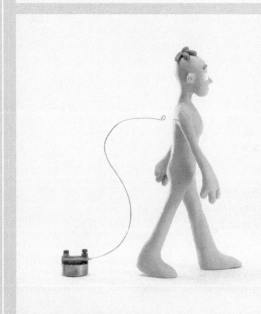

An animation curve rarely has even spacing. We have an increase in energy and speed at the start, and a decrease near the stop (see the chapter "Understanding and recreating motion," page 36).

On a curve, what we see is spacing (the distance between the animated object's poses) close together at the start (the motion starts slowly) that gradually gets further apart (the object gains speed) and, ultimately, gets closer again (the object slows down and comes to a stop):

If the stop is abrupt compared to the speed generated, for example, because of an impact against an obstacle, the object will bounce back in the opposite direction.

This bounce implies that the object may potentially end up in the same position as the last pose before the impact, just one or two frames later. If the frame just before the impact and the frame just after the impact are the same, the impact itself, which will only last one or two frames, may look like a flash, like a subliminal image between these two poses. To prevent this, we must be sure to place these two frames in different places on each side of the point of impact and space them differently with regard to the impact itself. For example, we'll place the last pose before impact farther away (the speed is still high prior to impact), and the first rebound pose close to the point of impact (the speed has suddenly lost its energy because of the obstacle).

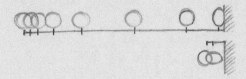

TIP!

When an animation curve eases out with a lot of very subtle spacing, the last space can be almost imperceptible and placed in the other direction.

Animation students are commonly asked to do the bouncing ball exercise. This presents the concept of the animation curve in a very simple way, with the curve's shape and spacing (it also introduces the concept of stretching and squashing, but, here, we will only talk about the curve).

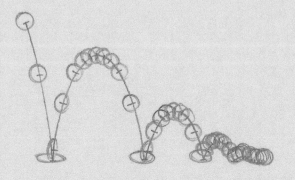

EXERCISE

What do animation curves tell us?

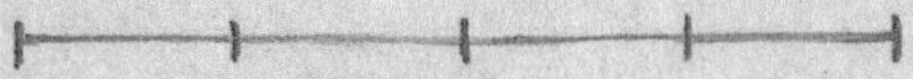

Answer

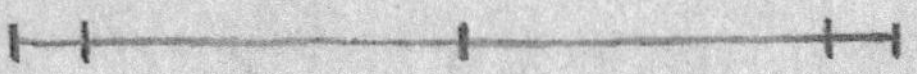

Answer

Answer

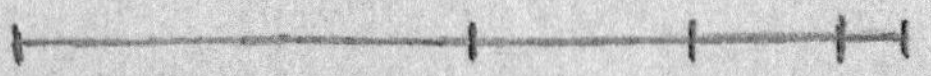

Answer

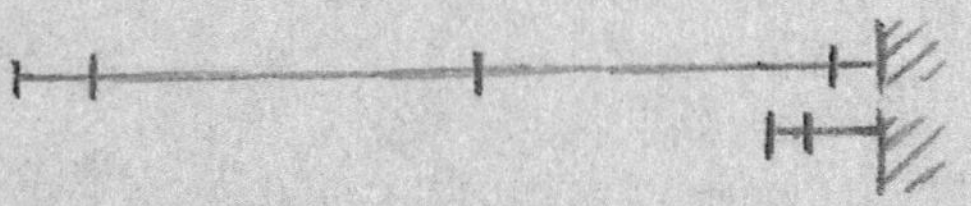

Answer

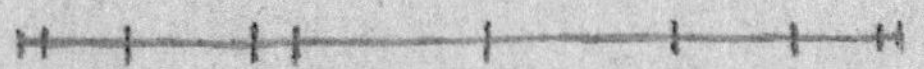

Answer

See the solutions at the end of the book.

A body that falls and bounces is made up of many bouncing balls, each with their own curve: the shoulders, the back, the pelvis, the legs, etc. They are all out of sync with each other because the energy source, the impact, and the effects from the movement of other parts of the body do not arrive at each body part at the same time.

Too even a spacing from one shape to another lessens the impact of strong actions and the motion's fluidity. Even spacing tends to create an animation as weak as a passing toy train. If we wish to create dynamic animation, we need strong gestures that contrast with the character's overall pacing. The inbetweens must, therefore, be close to the extremes, like this:

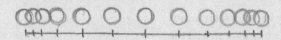

As opposed to like this:

> SOME CONSIDERATIONS TO KEEP IN MIND REGARDING THE CAMERA

When a camera is in motion, one can very easily be fooled into thinking there is movement, even though your animated element is not moving at all. Do not allow yourself to be influenced by this! After a number of frames, you will notice your eye is seeing perfectly well that the character, in the motion's follow-through, has stopped moving early or abruptly. Do not put too much trust in what the camera is showing in this particular scenario. Rely, above all, on the memory of your gesture, your experience and any points of reference (marks on the ground, stopwatch time, etc.) as a guide to determine the right timing for the action. Whatever the case may be, and when in doubt, it is always better to slow an action too much than not enough when dealing with camera movements.

Camera movements have animation curves separate from the movement of the animated element in the scene. Unless the camera is attached to the animated element, and unless it is a subjective camera (like a GoPro), as soon as the element is filmed by an outside camera, this outside camera's movement (if any) is independent and totally its own, as if a cameraman was holding it in their hands.

If the element in the scene comes to a sudden stop (with a rebound or another type of sudden cushioning), the camera in motion following it does not undergo the same sudden stop. It reacts independently, depending on what is conveyed: it can slow down very quickly (with gradually tighter spacing) until it comes to a complete stop, it can slow down with a bounce – in the same way as the object being filmed or with multiple bounces (camera shake), etc.

Watch out! For a close-up, we will need more cushioning to get the same fluid effect as we will for a wide shot. A head turning in a close-up stops in eight to ten poses, while in a long shot the same head will stop in perhaps three poses.

CHEATS AND FIXES

A mistake in straight-ahead animation can be really bad news if it means you have to remove numerous frames and redo the bad part and all the frames after it.

Unfortunately, if you see a mistake, it is very likely someone else sees it too. If you are working on a very high-quality production, the mistake must be corrected: go back to the bad frame, reset the elements and redo the animation from that frame forward. If it is a production with a budget that doesn't allow you to correct such imperfections, you must first ask yourself whether the mistake is situated in the center of the action (where the viewer is looking). If this is not the case, if the mistake is only visible when you look at it and is not in the viewer's zone of focus, we can sometimes leave it be. If it is in the viewer's zone of focus, we have to consider what options we have and then decide what's best to do.

✕ Is the viewer going to see it/be jarred/notice there's a hitch? The frame must always be redone if there is a risk the viewer will notice it.

✕ Are you the only one who knows there is a mistake (for example, because it does not fit with what you had in mind for the scene, even though overall it's okay)? If this is the case, is it possible for you to redo something in a way that won't be jarring to the viewer? If you are working on a personal or semi-amateur project, you will often have this possibility.

✕ If you're on a professional production, is it likely the director and other people will discover that it's a mistake? If this is the case, you'll need to talk with the director and decide whether or not to redo it.

Animation Curve Mistakes

In animation, a frame on an animation curve is considered a mistake (also referred to as a "hitch") in the following three scenarios:

× We forgot to animate one element out of a group. A pose freezes for four or more frames while an animated element is fully in motion.

× It deviates from the trajectory. There is a gap in our animation curve: one or more of the object's points do not follow the trajectory harmoniously.

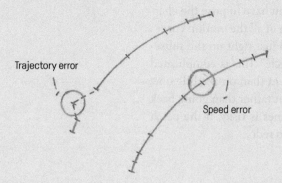

Trajectory error

Speed error

× The speed is uneven. The object is on the right trajectory, but we have a spacing that is too big or too small in the follow-through. This also applies to slow-in and slow-out: if the spacing gets gradually closer to slow down the stop, and then begins to get farther apart again, we have the same issue, inconsistent speed.

What are the solutions?

The solutions in key-frame animation require very little effort. We are not directly under the camera. The animator is not forced to follow the scene's chronological order, regardless of the objects (characters). It's a matter of simply modifying the bad frames; the rest of the animation, if everything works all right, doesn't need changing.

In straight-ahead animation, a mistake means that we have to go back to the bad frame, delete everything that comes after it – even if it's good – and reshoot the deleted frames. Often, we try to avoid reaching this point by using some tricks and tips. Indeed, we can correct a mistake by cheating a little or by changing its initial intent.

× For example, if it's an oversight, we can try to pull out the frozen frame and see if the animation looks fluid after its removal, or if that causes a jump in speed. This solution is usually not an option when there are other animated elements in the scene at the same time, but sometimes we can get lucky.

× For an omission on the previous image, and in the event there is a deviation in the motion (an omission affecting the spacing during the cushioning), we can try to restart on this new animation curve, in the opposite direction, like a bounce, or in a new direction, if it seems warranted for the action.

✕ For a mistake that is impossible to fix, for example if we've animated an element toward the left on two frames and have forgotten to animate it thereafter, going back over the animation once we've noticed it by continuing to animate it to the left and leaving the still images in the middle may actually aggravate the mistake and make it more visible. On the other hand, we can try to leave the mistake around eight to ten frames and animate the element in the other direction (to the right, in this case), being careful to make an impeccable, fluid and smooth animation curve from that point on.

✕ Another solution is to insert fixes in the middle of the shot (what I refer to as a "patch"). We can occasionally try to correct a passage when we've completely finished the scene. Such a feat is complicated and often impossible; not only do you have to pose the character just right to match the follow-through of all the motion curves up to that point, but you also have to land just right on the subsequent curve when coming out of the "patch." This is complicated and usually works better on a big movement than on a subtle one. The notion of completely finishing the shot rather than going back and fixing without deleting too many frames is risky. If the patch doesn't work, there will be a lot of frames to redo.

A few ways of cheating...

Some small tricks make it possible to get through a hard-to-animate movement.

✕ Sometimes, the puppet or the set does not permit a particular motion, for example, one that is very big or subtle. In this scenario, animate another part of the body, or a part of the set in the object's immediate surroundings, at the same time. The secondary motion will give the primary motion an illusion of subtlety, precision or breadth by its mere presence in the field of vision and will divert attention from the technical difficulties on the primary element. You can, for example, use an animal's tail to "fluidify" the perception of the whole.

✕ By the same logic, when animating a rather erratic or abrupt movement (a character walking very fast intended to make the viewer laugh, for example), try to at least have a stable or flexible part that the eye can lock onto (for example, the head).

The head remains relatively still, while the hands move.

✕ When we absolutely have to achieve a certain shape or arrive at a specific point at the end of a shot, animating in reverse order might be a good solution, if the animation is simple and if there are no other animated elements in the shot. This is the case, for example, for a piece of paper that unfolds that has to have a perfect shape at the end of the shot, for a simple ball that transforms into a dragon, or for an object that rolls up to a specific spot in the scenery.

Transforming a ball into a complex
dragon is difficult if we animated in
the order of the images. Here, we
cheat and animate it in reverse order:
from the detailed dragon
to the simple ball.

Loops

Loops are animations that repeat endlessly; the first frames have the same follow-through as the last frames, making it impossible to distinguish between the first and last frame.

X One trick for making loops without making the loop point noticeable is to always place this point where the interval in the animation curve changes the most. If we place the hookup point on the most subtle interval, aligning the end of the loop becomes very complex. The first and last frames are, thus, the poses where the change is the most pronounced, so as to hide the hookup in the motion's magnitude.

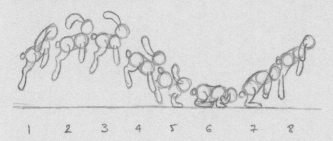

X Another trick for making good loops is to camouflage the repetition from being read by the viewer. I call this "smart loops." We animate two or three loops as identical as possible, then we "collect" frames for our subsequent loops at random from the three hand-animated loops, thus avoiding repetitions.

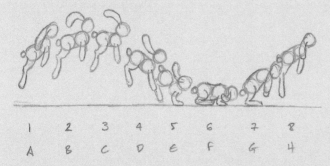

The poses of the jumping rabbit are numbered from 1 to 7 for the first cycle, then A to G for the second cycle. These two cycles are animated entirely under the camera, with the pose 1 being the same as pose A. Pose A will come right after pose 7. When making a smart loop, we mix the frames from the first cycle (1-7) with the frames from the second cycle (A-G) somewhat at random. For example, like this:

Frame number	1	2	3	4	5	6	7	8	9	10	11	12	13	14	15	16	17	18	...
Pose name	1	B	C	4	E	6	7	A	2	3	D	5	F	G	A	B	3	4	...

▶ **Create a loop!**

Animate some apples endlessly falling on a character's head. Here, we animate a single apple falling and loop it to achieve a never-ending action.

Replacement Animation

Replacement animation consists of physically creating a copy of the animated element for each pose of its movement.

This little trick is frequently and widely used (even by the biggest studios on the most prestigious projects). It is even a legitimate animation technique, halfway between stop motion and cartoon, where each pose is sketched on a piece of paper before being created then captured by the camera. Look up the works of George Pal: you'll discover some very famous examples and very impressive animations produced exclusively using replacement.

This is about saving modeling time by preparing copies of the element in advance, one copy per pose. Next, we work on each copy of the element in the required pose. Then, once we've worked on the whole set of poses and are ready to film, all we have to do is replace the element in place with its copy in the following pose, which in turn will be replaced by the following copy, and so on and so forth. In this way, we avoid modeling one element into very similar poses, but we also avoid taking risks if the animation involves a complex or irreversible action.

Below, for example, we have a snack munched through frame by frame: the cracker is broken in a way that is very hard to control, whereas, for its part, the cheese has to show teeth marks sculpted by hand so that they are easier to read and more harmonious. These two variables are far too unpredictable to attempt an animation on the spot. Thus, we opt to create multiple copies of crackers and cheese in advance and adapt them one after another according to the poses desired in the sequence.

We very often find replacement animations in walking, running and jumping cycles to avoid modeling the same poses each cycle: if an animation has four cycles of a jump that consists of five distinct poses, we'll have to sculpt thirty-two animation poses. Thanks to our pre-sculpted phases, the work is reduced to modeling five poses.

The time-saving logic applies to syncing lips with dialogue as well (*lip-sync*): productions generally opt for replacement mouths that avoid sculpting and re-sculpting the same mouth from one frame to the next.

UNDERSTANDING AND DEPICTING MOTION

To understand how to obtain an animation curve with accurate and justified direction and speed, we're going to look at how motion works, where it comes from and how it behaves. Then, we'll see how these rules influence our animations.

ENERGY SOURCES AND THEIR EFFECTS

Energy always has a source somewhere. Any body, like any object, is in motion thanks to an energy source that has been applied to it, whether internally (our muscles contract and move our arms) or externally (the hand pushes a tissue over a table's edge and gravity makes it fall to the floor).

Desynchronization

No body (or object) moves all of its elements at the same time. Not only is this not true to the physics of motion, but we would also lose visual information on the screen. Therefore: desynchronize! There is always an element that begins moving before another, whether it's due to the physics of energy transfer and chain reactions or whether it's due to a train of thought and its physical manifestations.

— The transfer of energy from one element can set another element in motion. The arm moves the hand, which moves the fingers, and, on the other extremity, the arm also moves the torso, which moves the head and other parts of the body.

— We can also show a train of thought through a sequence of physical expressions: an action can be placed on a primary element, such as eyes squinting in suspicion, and then move to a secondary element, such as the eyebrows. Another part of the face is going to move a fraction of second later with its own expressive gesture: the mouth will pucker up. It is not set into motion automatically by the skin, but it nevertheless performs its own meaningful action and increases the perception of the face's expression as a whole. The train of thought reaches different parts of the body at different times. Non-verbal communication (body language) is unsynchronized, and it is very important to know where motion is delayed following a previous action.

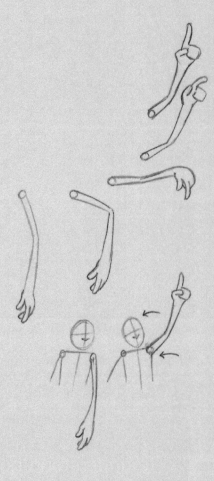

A key to high-quality animation lies in these secondary animations, which are a product of a primary motion. Understanding (and animating!) the motions generated by secondary elements after a primary element's is quite often the quality that separates a very good animator from a less meticulous one. When this understanding is there, the animation is less stiff.

TIP!

Lightly touching surface of some fabric or modeling clay can be enough to create an illusion of a living body in which everything is interconnected, but also a transfer of energy.

EXERCISES

▶ **Let us consider some moving toes – the big toe and the second toe – as a gesture that expresses excitement.**

What are the primary and secondary actions?

Answer

▶ **Let's try a yawn (but exaggerated, with the arms stretched out).**

What are the primary and secondary actions?

Answer

See the solutions at the end of the book.

✕ Chain of priorities

Establishing a chain of priorities isn't just a sure way to not forget an element from among the many you have to handle, it especially helps make the motion more physically accurate and logical, too. It's like building the internal volumes in a drawing. You can try to draw just the immediately visible part and trust your instinct, but to be sure of your choices, especially if you don't have much experience, it is wiser to lay a solid foundation and build up from there. In drawing, this foundation is the volume; in animation, the foundation is the source of the motion, then the chain reaction, element by element.

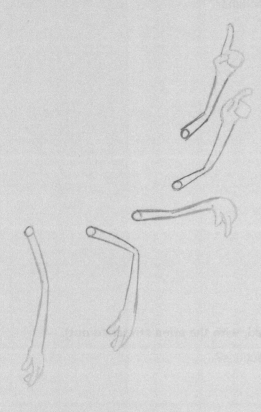

— **The primary part (in blue):** this is the priority. This must be animated, no matter your intentions. This is the driving force behind the motion.

— **The secondary parts (here, in green):** these are easy to forget between the primary and tertiary parts. If we don't animate them, the motion will be very stiff, lacking life and realism. In the above example, if the forearm in green wasn't animated with a delay, the elbow would look like it's stuck, or like it's not even there at all. The arm would move like a stick, devoid of fluidity and grace.

The secondary parts follow the primary's' energy, at all times like the above example. The arm is our primary part (in blue), through the elbow, which is an extension of it, connects to the forearm (green), which moves after it with a bit of a delay. Subsequently, we slow our secondary animations when the primary animation is stopped or is about to stop.

— **The tertiary parts:** these are surprisingly more animated than the secondary parts because they're on the extremities and are more visible **(in yellow)**. These are going to make the difference between a stiff, lower quality animation, and a good one. They bring it to life. But be careful not to "over-animate" them compared to the secondary parts. In the illustration, the hand, in yellow, will be the final touch that animates the arm, however it will also be the finishing line and destination of the motion as a whole.

TAKE NOTE!

Developing this arm movement is just an example, of course, but there is nothing stopping you from showing a finger lifting up in a more intentional, less casual manner and, thus, choosing a driving element different from this example for one action. It's all a question of intent; the energy sources must be placed in an intelligent, well-thought manner.

✕ When the whole body is in action, like during a sports activity, it is often easier to animate by starting at the hips and following the energy's path through the rest of the body, element by element.

✕ If just the head (or the top part of the body) is in action, do not forget that the transfered energy and the motion affect the entire body, as subtle as the effect may be.

✕ Similarly, we do not move all the elements in the same direction. The element generating the energy can cause an element to move in the other direction. If we take a lasso, for example, the arm rotates and makes the object spin, and we notice that its effect on the body's motion moves the torso back and forth in the opposite direction of the arm. When the arm moves toward the body, the torso moves toward the arm, and when the arm moves away from the body, the torso moves away from the arm.

✕ Another example: a person juggling a soccer ball.

Analyze the sense of balance (the body uses leverage to compensate for the weight of the outstretched leg) and the chain reaction (the whole body reacts to the leg in action to maintain the center of gravity under control).

✕ The direct transfer of energy and "sharing" the animation curve is common, and it is important to understand them. In action, object A comes into direct contact with object B and involves it in its own animation curve, thus transferring its energy (and therefore the direction of its motion and its speed) to object B, which will continue the curve, even if A changes direction. For example, a ball thrown by an arm. The ball does not have its own initial movement on its animation curve. The arm takes care of that. The ball begins its curve at full speed because it was sharing the arm's animation curve before being released.

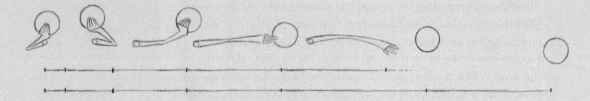

Inertia

Inertia is a very important principle in animation. It corresponds to the time needed for the motion started by the force at the energy source to come to a stop. This time depends on a number of factors, such as the motion's speed, the weight, the friction exerted on the object. If we run really fast and try to stop, we will need certain amount of time to slow down and stop completely because we only have our muscles to exert an opposing force allowing us to stop. On the other hand, a canvass bag sliding on the ground in the street after being tossed will come to a stop rather quickly from the friction against the asphalt.

✕ The energy source plays a big role in inertia and the order in which different elements are affected. The best example is the animation of a rhythmic gymnastics ribbon because we see the energy physically move up and down the object, which allows us to create the curves and whirls common to the aesthetic of this sport. The energy comes from the gymnast's arm and travels toward the hand, then ribbon's handle, and lastly the ribbon itself, point by point for the full length of it.

✕ If we stop suddenly (for example, because of a root that creates an obstacle), the elements closest to the source of the stop will be the first to stop (the feet, of course, then the legs), and the ones furthest away will have greater inertia (the upper part of the body, then the head, and lastly the arms).

Let's take a bus with people inside as an example: the bus' wheels stop; the bus is thrust forward a bit. The same thing happens to the people inside the bus: the upper part of the body goes further than the lower part, which is in contact with the bus by way of the floor or the seats.

✕ Any object takes some time to start and stop moving. There is no standard number of ease-in and ease-out poses, just as there is not standard cruising speed for an action. Certain people are very dynamic, others are rather nonchalant. The same person can move slowly and steadily at first, then quickly and energetically later in the scene. There is no rule: these are always decisions that depend on the moment and the circumstances of the shot.

Are we in an animation curve of a slow, steady traditional train that can stop rather quickly?

Or are we closer to an animation curve for a new high-speed train that requires longer to slow down and stop?

✕ Careful, however, not to kill your effects: if the motion is extremely fast, like an excited dog's wagging tail (a tail that will be animated with two images on one side, two on the other), do not hesitate to freeze the tail's internal joints. Do not give the animation too much flexibility. In fact, we must avoid twisting the shape into multiple curves in order to show the delay in the energy that propagates throughout the tail, like we would readily do with the gymnast's ribbon or a lion tamer's whip. On the other hand, in this case, consider this element to be rather rigid. On one hand, an animal's tail is not as flexible as we might think; on the other hand, here, the element's flexibility might visually weaken the motion's energy and action in the scene, as well. In this way, the impression of hyperactivity might be lost.

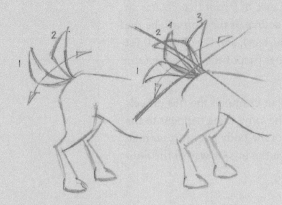

× What is the object's weight? You have to adapt your animation to this. Each object is subject to these laws, based on the weight, the height, the force applied, the opposing forces applied, etc. Therefore, when we animate, we determine all this to obtain the most accurate, most credible and most meaningful animation. An object that is very heavy will need much more inertia to displace its weight, much more inertia to start or stop a motion. An object that is very light may, on the other hand, bring about all these changes more suddenly.

The Rebound

A bouncing effect is an effect of inertia. The opposing force applied is such (for example, an obstacle that abruptly stops our arm) that the element's inertia must express itself by going in the opposite direction. Let's think of a ball bouncing on the ground (the obstacle it encounters) or Son Goku hurling a super-powerful ball of energy at his enemy in the series *Dragon Ball Z*.

Let's take the example of an object that twists on itself when it bounces, such as thunder sheet (sheet metal noise-makers use to recreate the sound of thunder, for example). The stopping obstacle is the very limit of the object's body.

Here is what we have: a maximum curvature to the right, a nearly straight inbetween, slightly to the left, then a maximum curvature to the left, a return inbetween curved to the left, a return inbetween curved to the right, then nearly straight to the left, and nearly straight to the right, imperceptibly straight toward the left, imperceptibly straight toward the right, completely straight, and lastly an ever-so subtle or slight movement.

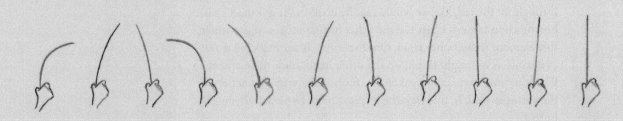

Anticipations

When we start an animation curve (i.e. a motion) very quickly, very abruptly and very dynamically, we have to prepare it by placing an anticipation. This is usually animated in the opposite direction of the main action, in order to build up energy before suddenly releasing it. Think of a rubber band you stretch in one direction that takes off like an arrow in the other direction when you let it go, or a spring that your flatten all the way down that suddenly decompresses and shoots upward when you lift your hand.

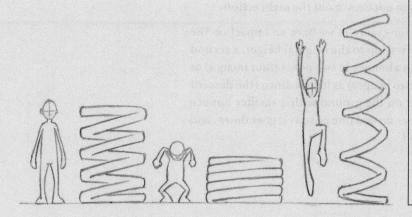

TAKE NOTE!

One can create a comical effect even without anticipation. For example, the Road Runner, the famous cartoon character, takes off like a shot without showing any sign of accumulated energy right after he leaps in the air and sticks his tongue out mockingly. A cloud of smoke takes the character's place all of a sudden, from one image to the next. This action is clearly distinct from that of his archenemy, Wile E. Coyote, who always takes off very fast after an exaggerated, squashed anticipation in the opposite direction.

If the main action is very big and fast, we place the anticipation in the opposite direction on four or six frames; if it is moderately big and fast, we can have an anticipation on two images. This is just a rule of thumb, but, to summarize, the more sudden and dynamic the action, the longer and more exaggerated the anticipation. How big the anticipation is depends on how big the action is, itself.

Cushioning

Cushioning stops motion naturally. A stop can be fast, even very fast, but the cushioning is nevertheless there.

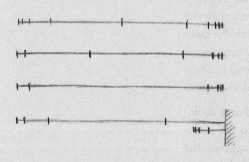

These animation curves show the dynamics of the movements and their respective ease-ins/outs. They change from motion at a constant speed to an abrupt, dynamic impact and finish with a cushioning after a rebound.

The more extreme the motion, the higher the number of cushioning poses.

Dealing with the last pose of cushioning can sometimes be a delicate task. The last interval should be virtually invisible to the eye.

TIP!

Placing a blinking eye on the last pose of your character's softening can help the viewer read the motion's stop more smoothly.

Occasionally, the last pose before stopping is not a pose. We just run a finger over the character, and this barely noticeable change is enough.

> FALLING OBJECTS

We do not want objects to distract from the scene's main action and draw attention away from the character. Objects that fly, fall, etc. must, therefore, be impeccably executed so that the viewer doesn't "see them without seeing them," so that a fall that wouldn't be natural doesn't draw the viewer's attention. However, rather insignificant secondary objects must also come to a stop rather quickly after impact so as to not drown out the main action.

Let's take a falling chair, for example: we have an impact on the ground and a bounce halfway up to the original height, a second impact on the ground with a bounce in two poses (four images) as it goes up and one pose (two images) as it goes down (the descent is faster), then an impact on the ground with a smaller bounce with just one pose as it goes up and one pose as it goes down, and lastly a stop on the ground.

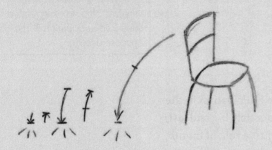

Secondary Action
vs. Primary Action

An element in motion can be classified into two types of actions: its movement can be the source of the action (primary) or it can be generated by another source (this is a secondary action, as we saw on page 36). The primary action's movements affect the viewer differently than the secondary action's movements, even if they potentially touch the same part of the body. The direction the viewer attributes to the movement you depict may be the complete opposite of what you intend to show if you animate a primary action as a secondary action, and vice-versa.

✗ Let's take an involuntary laugh, for example: The head and shoulders lift up and move lightly and quickly in reaction to the abdomen, which is the source. Here, it isn't necessary to exaggerate the elbows' movement as if they were controlled and had their own energy source. They need to be animated in reaction to the shoulders' movements. They must not distract us or give us the sense that the character is overacting or hamming it up.

✗ Now, let's imagine a forced laugh. The viewer instinctively knows that the laugh is forced because the secondary animations are no longer a reaction to the primary animations at the energy source, at the inflated abdomen. There is no inflated abdomen because there is no reflexive laugh. There is only a semblance of a laugh, conveyed by different elements on the body shaking by force. The shaking should normally react to the source movement coming from the abdomen, but, in this case, they are moving without a source and are their own source of energy. The shoulders, for example, lift up exaggeratedly to make the laugh artificial.

✕ With a jump on a bed, we have everything: a fall, a soft surface cushioning the fall, a bounce transferring energy to the springs in the mattress, and even secondary animations (the legs, the mattress, the hair, etc.) and primary animations, which are going to provide the source of energy and continue the action indefinitely (the arms in motion do not move as a reaction but of their own free will to add energy and force to the rest of the body, to perpetuate the overall movement). We even have weight differences if several characters are jumping and have different body shapes (the lightest is going to bounce a little higher than the heaviest).

Thus, here the character is falling downward with increasingly greater spacing and is stopped suddenly by the bed; next, the bed is squashed as it cushions the fall, followed by a bounce in the opposite direction right after. On contact, all the moving elements on the character's body are still in the air trailing behind the fall (and are out of sync with the energy source all the way to the furthest moving element). On the rebound image, when the mattress moves upward, the body's moving parts are still falling and out of sync with the body, which is in direct contact with the energy source and bouncing upward. Meanwhile, the arms, which want to inject their own energy into the overall motion to continue the action indefinitely, are less delayed and less out of sync.

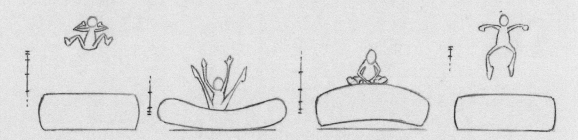

EXERCISES

▶ **Animate a character rummaging through a cardboard box full of papers.**

▶ **Animate a character bailing water out of a boat.**

See the solutions at the end of the book.

Unless you've been hired for a film with a predetermined style, find your own voice, especially if it's a personal project. Don't animate like other people, rather animate what you see, what you feel is right.

Michael Dudok de Wit, for example, did not animate the birds in the film *Le Moine et le Poisson* (The Monk and the Fish) with great big graceful wings like herons or pigeons. Being sparrows, these birds were animated as such. These are little black dots in the sky that flap their wings frenetically and glide for a few moments before flapping them again. If he had animated the birds in a conventional manner, we would have recognized them as birds, but without any specific context. Here, we recognize sparrows, and we perceive the time of day, the weather, the place and a sense of delicacy, of lightness that accompanies the rest of the film.

There is a reason for everything. Your style gives your animation a direction, a voice, whether it's the whole project or whether it's a particular character that contrasts with another.

Dynamism in Animation

The life, interest and personality of a film stems in great part from its dynamism. Avoid monotony. You lose the viewer because the story comes off flat, one-dimensional and lifeless, unless this is precisely the atmosphere you want to create.

X Create contrast! It makes the reading of the action easier. If an object is always moving erratically, we no longer see anything, we no longer make out the important actions. Conversely, but for the same reasons, if the pacing is too constant, too linear or too slow, it makes reading the action impossible and puts the viewer to sleep. If the pacing lacks dynamism, meaningful actions will get lost within all the neutral ambient moments.

For example, anticipate a big moment where a character smiles and the mouth has to open wide. For this smile, the mouth will have to be shut at other moments in order to create a contrast. By the same logic, take care to anticipate and gauge where to place your eyebrows. They should be at a neutral height during your neutral moments, while still achieving the right expression. This way, they will be able to take the expression to its highest or lowest point during big moments. If they are already placed at their highest point during a neutral moment, you won't be able to move them any higher during a particularly important moment, a big moment. To summarize, place your eyebrows in a way that fits the expression without, however, preventing yourself from creating contrast during a big moment.

The eyebrows were already higher than the neutral pose and, thus, don't have anywhere to go on the surprise pose.

The eyebrows can lift up on the surprise pose.

✗ The age, weight and overall personality of a character are factors that play a role in its dynamic. By avoiding stereotypes associated with these factors, we can create contrast and unexpected situations that will a have a big impact on the viewer.

✗ Do not be afraid of extreme motions (see the sequence at the bottom of this page). The key to their effectiveness lies in the anticipations and the cushioning. You need to signal the motion with a fluid anticipation (i.e. with very precise, progressive curves) that is proportionate to what is going to follow. Then, your cushioning needs to be just as fluid, even if its range of movement is limited and over just a few intermediate frames, like with a controlled, blocked stop.

A very dynamic body element with a controlled stop over very few intermediate frames still has an effect on the rest of the body, which, for its part, will be animated more subtly and smoothly.

✗ Desynchronize actions so that actions don't start and stop on the same image (see "Desynchronization," page 36).

✗ Vary the timing of your animation curves so that your big, dynamic movements have a greater impact on the viewer and so that these movements don't get drowned out by a flood of erratic actions.

Create contrast with smooth, subtle curves.

✕ To the extent possible, it is also important to introduce all the elements that will enter into action on screen as early as the anticipation phase, or earlier if possible, so that spots of light don't appear and disappear like a flash.

For example, a hand that would normally be off camera: here, we have the possibility to make it enter without compromising how the acting is viewed. During the anticipation, it is prepared over several anticipation poses in the opposite direction, just like the rest of the body (like we saw on page 43, with the image of the spring we compressed and suddenly released). When the extreme motion arrives and the hand moves across the screen in three frames, the spectators eyes are able to follow it because they had read it on the screen just prior.

TIP!

If you fear it will be too jarring, animate an object around it smoothly and fluidly, an element that doesn't draw attention but rather offsets the sudden, extreme dynamism. Trust in reality and in the physics of the movements: try these extreme movements!

Avoid

Correct

✕ When an action occurs quickly with a lot of energy, it can be tricky to get the cushioning right without losing the movement's dynamism. It feels like the cushioning poses are too numerous, too long. They become terribly tricky to animate without actually being superfluous; stopping here would be too abrupt, but slowing in with more poses would appear to weaken everything overall. In this scenario, there are many solutions that may help:

— when easing a rebound, the return spacing in the opposite direction can begin after four stable frames on the extreme position

preceding the return, instead of starting immediately after the usual two frames;

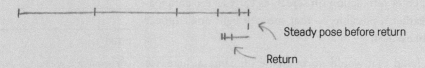

Steady pose before return

Return

— at the last interval, or even at the first stable pose, placing an eye blink or similar distraction will help stop the movement without giving the sense that the image is frozen;

— the very last cushioning pose (the one that we'll hardly be able to manipulate because it's so small) can be made easier by trying to replace the character exactly where it was; the very subtle, inevitable shift will be enough to make a perfect cushion;

— we can also place the last interval, very subtly on a bounce, on just one pose.

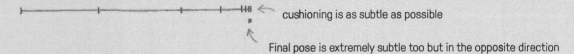

cushioning is as subtle as possible

Final pose is extremely subtle too but in the opposite direction

Realism vs. Cartoons

Cartoons hook viewers to the story thanks to many effects relying on exaggeration and surprise that can particularly – although not necessarily – cause a comic reaction.

Realistic animation, on the other hand, brings the viewer into the story with empathy, a mirror image effect, and a feeling of watching something tangible and concrete from real life.

Realistic animation

Realistic animation requires us to make extremely close observations. It reproduces movements, shapes and speed as real to life as possible. There is no exaggeration, it is accurate and precise. This accuracy and precision propels the viewer into the heart of the action. The world you give the viewer to see is their world. And, yet, it isn't because the viewer is watching an animation. This paradox can have a big impact on the viewer's perception and their emotions.

X Use video and mirrors to analyze the motion in close detail and observe the motion on a loop to feel the choreography and analyze it frame by frame (if you have a video of the motion) to determine not only the exact order of the energy transfers, but also the motion curves and their velocity.

X Use video resources on the Internet to access movements you cannot reproduce yourself or which you do not have access to.

X Observing daily life must become a constant mental exercise, just as the sketch pad becomes essential for an illustrator in daily life. Observe, observe, observe! People, animals, objects, elements of nature, etc. Everything is fair game for a small mental note (or a physical one, if you have something to note it down with) to supply your future animations: the little old lady is trying to cross the street somehow before the crosswalk light turns red; she's hurrying, even though it's very slow. What visual cues tell us she's hurrying if we can't tell by her actual speed? The man who just now came into the bar, what tells you he's here to meet someone he doesn't know? The child, like all children, runs differently than an adult. In what ways? A carton of milk falls from a shelf in the store but doesn't burst open: it got squashed some, but did it bounce? Did it bounce a little? Or not at all?

× A realistic animation does not disregard the rules of desynchronization and contrast. We've just touched on observing energy movement in real life, but also observe the role contrasts play in visual storytelling in films made using real shots with real flesh-and-blood actors.

Cartoon-style animation

Exaggeration is the trademark of cartoon-style animation. It has it all: motion curve, volume, creative content, speed.

Perform the action yourself with your own body, or ask a colleague to perform the action for you, then analyze the movements as you would for a realistic animation.

The cartoon version of a given movement is the same, except it's an exaggeration – and impossible if we're talking about the squashing, the stretching (*squash and stretch*), the twisting, or the spinning.

> *SQUASH AND STRETCH*

This principle is used very frequently; it's one of the fundamental rules. Therefore, to make high-quality animations, it's important that we understand it. This effect relies simultaneously on the energy and volume movement, and exaggerated distortions.

While the body moves in space, we're going to stretch its shape so as to physically show the delay between the reactive part and the active part (which is leading the movement).

Then, on impact or when the movement stops, we squash the shape by moving its volume to the side to show the delay. In fact, the parts that haven't yet been touched by the stop continue to move. This squashing or delaying effect on matter in motion can be seen in real life, particularly if we watch slow-motion videos: when in motion, skin (or another flexible part of the body) stretches and, all the more evidently, squashes. In cartoon-style animation, we consider the animated object's entire shape to be soft and flexible. We will automatically forget there is a skeleton, frame, or any other element to slow or stop motion. We will radically transform the whole shape and exaggerate it. Attention, however, we always conserve the object's volume, regardless of its shape: an object's volume moves but does not disappear!

Quick movements with an impact are among the most common elements, but this effect is applicable to an incalculable number of situations, such as an anticipation (a squashed spring effect) before an action (released spring/explosive effect), or all the "small" partial movements that can be considered a motion (stretching) with a stop (squashing).

✕ We can also exaggerate and play with the rules governing energy sources and their effects (pages 36-45) The example of the bounce on the mattress where the object gets squashed more than its initial pose (page 45) can be used in odd situations for an effective comical elastic effect.

✕ When animating, just when you think a pose is as extreme as it can get, try to go further. It will often be possible, and it's just the fear of going too far or changing the character too radically, or, with straight-ahead animation, not being able to go back and find a way out of the movement, that holds you back.

✕ Be brave! Even if the movement might take more animation or modeling time, it's worth it! This is your big moment, the one you animated all the movements leading up to it, with such restraint, to make it stand out by accentuating its impact. The viewer is ready, you signaled the extent of motion with the right amount of anticipation, you can now go further and make the comical effect immediately easier to read and, thus, more effective at generating laughs. If you squash, squash it even flatter! If you stretch, stretch it even longer! If you twist, twist it even tighter!

✕ Do not drown your big pose in a sequence of other motions. You need to keep it in place for a moment or two with very closely spaced intervals so that the viewer doesn't just have time to read it but also enjoy it a little (within what's reasonable and without abandoning the action's overall dynamic.) To illustrate the importance of holding big poses, think of some very popular low-budget productions, such as Japanese manga. Most of these series have virtually no animation (of movements) and rely almost completely on powerful still poses that tremble, that are moved slowly across the screen, or are enhanced by low-budget albeit very powerful effects (for example, adding speed lines or flashing color backgrounds).

Let's look at some cartoon animation motions.

✕ **Chewing food:** the lower the head goes, the more the cheeks fill with chewed food; the jaws are closed. The more the head goes up, the cheeks deflate; the jaws relax and the food moves in the mouth.

✕ **Whistling:** sometimes, a cartoon animation (the most traditional) is not just an exaggerated version of a real movement, it is also the viewer's perception of a movement that has always been depicted in a certain way. For example, we inflate the character's cheeks when it chews or catches its breath, which seems perfectly normal when compared to real life, and it also makes sense for a character's cheeks to be inflated when whistling, however... Try to whistle and you'll notice your cheeks go inward instead of the opposite. When you pucker your lips to whistle, the jaw is open, and it automatically draws in the cheeks by stretching the skin. The minuscule cheek movements are not simply the result of air going in and out, they are also produced by the tongue's squashing and stretching movements inside the mouth to create the tones. Nevertheless, the image most widely accepted by viewers to depict a whistling movement, and thus the image perpetuated in animation to this day, remains inflated cheeks moving to the music. The viewer would not understand the action as easily without this visual code.

WATCH OUT!

A cartoon animation often goes hand in hand with an exaggerated design and can change the weight and energy distribution rules: for example, a very big head on a small, slender body.

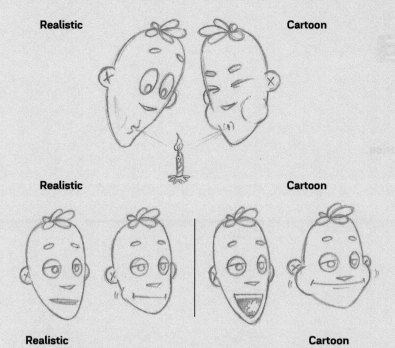

Realistic   **Cartoon**

Realistic   **Cartoon**

Realistic   **Cartoon**

✕ **Swallowing:** the mouth moves upward, then a ball appears on the throat while the mouth continues to move upward. The bulge gets bigger for two or three poses while the mouth's upward movement slows. Next, the mouth moves downward a little, and the ball is quickly swallowed and disappears. The mouth cushions the downward movement. Slightly moving the stomach gives the impression of movement inside the body.

> **TAKE NOTE!**
>
> We can add a small downward mouth anticipation before the initial pose (mouth upward) for a rounder, more exaggerated effect.

EXERCISE

▶ **Animate the surprise.**

In a realistic style:

In a cartoon style (exaggerated):

See the solutions at the end of the book.

Useful Materials

Here is a list of easily available, inexpensive materials that allow you to make some of the most popular and common special effects. Explore and remain curious about new materials in your daily life!

✕ **Plastic wrap** is quite often used for water effects (jet of water, spilled water, ripples on a surface, etc.

✕ **Hand sanitizer gel** is very good for depicting dripping/falling drops of water, but be careful: they evaporate quickly, which is both good and bad. You have to animate quickly and add more when necessary.

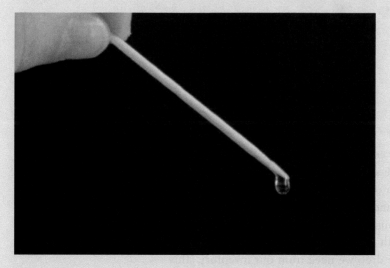

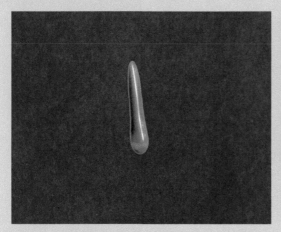
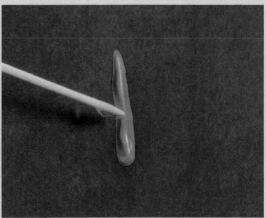

Any other totally transparent and rather "slow" (i.e. thick) gel can do the job, for example dish or hand soap. Find the best gel for you, your style and the scene, especially if there's a need for cleaning or invisible marks.

× **Plain transparent glue** is useful to create water drop effects or for continuously shiny surface (e.g. the tongue). It is not as easy to use as hand sanitizer gel, but it dries or evaporates less quickly. On the other hand, it does leave a film or residue. This can be useful for depicting drops of sweat that gradually appear and stay on the forehead because they are too small to run (for drops that get bigger and begin to drip, go back to hand sanitizer gel) and take a bit of time to evaporate. The slow evaporation means we have to animate straight ahead and be as consistent as we would with time-lapse. Indeed, if we take a break to have a coffee or a snack, when we get back, the glue will be much drier than it was before the break.

× **Hot glue** is also frequently used for drop effects. I don't use this very often because I don't like its opaque, yellowish color, but it is nevertheless popular with animators. It has the advantage that it allows us to prepare different drop and dripping phases in advance. Here we are making replacement animation (see page 31) by creating drops of the right size and length for each pose needed. When it's time to shoot, we just grab the drop we need from our inventory. This

method helps us get around the uncertainty associated with animating with hand sanitizer gel right in front of the camera.

× **Modeling Beeswax** is a material often used in stop-motion animation. It is easy to mold and very firm. We use it for spraying effects, trickling or stable liquids. The semi-transparent, off-yellow wax can be colored (there is no such thing as completely transparent wax). Its texture can look rather shiny on camera.

× **Aluminum** is used in particular to reflect light, for example the water's surface, by adjusting the sheet's moldable textures and wrinkles. We can also use it for fire (with red, yellow or orange aluminum): we cut it into shapes resembling flames and change them with each pose. We can also reflect and animate the light under wood logs to depict the embers in a fireplace. The possibilities are numerous.

× **Colored tissue paper or transparent plastic sheets** are also a good way to depict a fire effect, with, as you might imagine, much more transparency and nuanced color than aluminum. Tissue paper will reflect less light (it's slightly opaque), but the transparent plastic sheets can reflect a lot of light depending how you position them and the overall brightness. Thus, we can use tissue paper or colored transparent plastic sheets to achieve the same effects as the colored paper below, but with transparency as an added dimension, if appropriate.

TIP!

We also use modeling beeswax to harden modeling clay when it is too soft and, therefore, too difficult to animate. We use it especially for small elements that are often used but don't change their shape too much, like replacement eyelids. Thus, mix 10-20% wax to the modeling clay's volume and knead it until the mix is homogeneous (this is the reason we only use wax on small elements).

The more beeswax we add, the harder the modeling clay becomes. Nevertheless, it softens up quickly, particularly when we handle it a lot or it's used in a studio with a warmer than normal room temperature. Indeed, wax is much more "extreme" than modeling clay: it is harder when the temperature is average to cool, but softer when the temperature increases. If a frequently animated element, i.e. an element frequently warmed by the hands when handling it (e.g. mouths) contains too much wax, the element in question will get soft and sticky very quickly, and it will be hard to sculpt it right. On the other hand, if an infrequently handled or sculpted element (such as an eyelid we do little more than put on and take off) contains wax, this element will be very hard and retain its shape, assuming the studio temperature is cool to average. By contrast, a large amount of wax will make the element a little bit more shiny.

✕ **Colored paper** will depict visual effects close to cartoons.

— **Explosions.**

— **"Zaps."** Here, we reproduce a common cartoon effect by taking one (or more) pictures in the middle of the transformation process and incorporating funny, bizarre poses, or by depicting the element in an X-ray version, for example.

— **Lighting bolts, strobe effects** in a negative/positive sequence.

— **Motion blurs and smears** (see "Enhanced Perception," page 69).

Colored paper can thus be used for all sorts of special effects, in general, with a comical twist, but it is also totally possible to use it to create some more conventional special effects, such as fire, smoke or water, if the project's overall design allows for it.

✕ **Cotton** is good for making "clean" cloud/smoke effects: clouds in good weather, water vapor, steam, etc.

✕ **Steel wool**, on the other hand, is good for making the "dirty" version of clouds/smoke: rain, pollution, fire.

✕ In a modeling clay project, everything can be made using the same material. All the effects above, as well as many others, are moldable and always depend on the overall design:

— **drops of water or sweat;**

— **fire;**

— **smoke.**

On a production using hard materials (silicone, latex, resin, wood, etc.), **modeling clay** is very useful for:

— **thick, viscous, non-transparent splatters or runs** (mud, soup, sauce, a colored drink, mucus, etc.);

— **chewing gum, glue, or other elastic materials.**

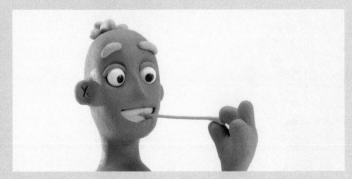

We can also use it for common illustration effects, such as blurs, smears, (see "Enhanced perception," page 69), and all the effects we cut out from paper. This is very enjoyable to make and incorporate in a scene, and all the more so because the viewer sense the originality without, however, being unsettled. Here's an explosion:

✕ The possibilities with materials are unlimited. Yarn, wool, cloth, wood, Christmas decorations, polystyrene, plastic wrapping, etc. So many elements present in your daily life can be perfectly inserted in your project!

A Few Animation Tips

Here is a set of specific tips for using these materials for special effects.

✕ If your character wipes away tears of laughter or sadness, think about making them appear ahead of time. In theory, this seems obvious and, yet, so often does the animator work, frame after frame, without thinking about what they will need to introduce for their main action a few seconds later.

✕ Animating with gel (or another thick liquid) live right on the spot can be tricky, risky even. I recommend animating the gel with a toothpick, which helps stretch the drop along the surface. We just add some more if we lose some as we go or if it evaporates. We lightly wipe away any streaks if we find they are too long on the back end, but in general the lack of gel on this spot usually helps things evaporate faster.

✕ Animate the drops of gel last in your sequence of manipulations. That's because this product can change very quickly.

✕ The trickiest, though also the most exhilarating, moment is capturing a drop in "full flight" as it falls down and hits the ground. This can sometimes require several attempts. After animating the rest of the scene, stretch the drop almost to the point where it will break off and fall, then, ready to shoot, wait for it to finish stretching into the perfect shape all on its own. For the next picture, the drop will obviously be on the ground, so you will need to add more gel and stretch the drop in place again for the following pose.

After that comes the fall, strictly speaking. Here, we wait and shoot when the drop breaks off. With any luck, we'll get a nice drop right as it falls. Otherwise, we'll delete the picture and put a drop back on the verge of falling.

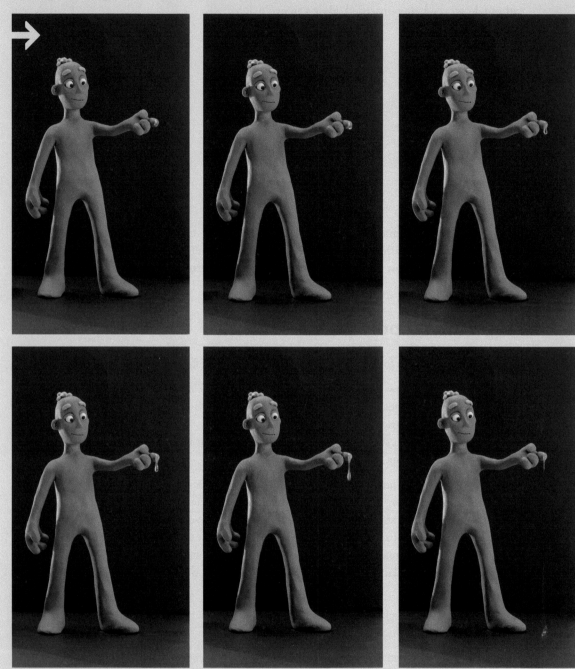

✗ If the drop is the image's only animated element, we can steadily take pictures as it stretches until it breaks off and falls.

✗ Will Becher, a fellow animator, shared this tip with his team one day: for the moment when the drop hits the surface, we make two butterflies, a big one and a small one, using stretchable film or a piece of transparent plastic packaging. We glue the small butterfly to the surface for the first image, then the big one in the same spot for the second image. After that, all we have to do is animate the water that drips after the impact, as explained on pages 63-64.

This effect works extremely well for rain; and this way, we can avoid the typical lines we see for rain in these kinds of scenes, which are hard to depict without the help of a computer.

✗ If capturing a drop of water as it falls isn't possible, or if we don't have some kind of support to hold a hard drop (made from hot glue or modeling clay) during its fall (no rig or background surface to affix the drop to mid-fall), we can totally forego this pose and pose the butterfly on the impact. The brain will create the mid-fall pose all by itself, and the effect will be just as realistic.

✗ For splashing water, we can use an aluminum wire to create the splash's shape and then fill it with gel if the surface is not too important. The aluminum wire will look like a reflection and will normally be invisible on screen. Animate the aluminum to animate the splash's shape, then rework the gel for each pose.

✕ To animate a flowing jet of water, we make several copies of the jet's shape using stretchable film, and in the middle of the film we make several folds with an wide base resembling blooming flower. Four or five copies of the same thickness are enough. We place one on the screen, then we replace it with another for the next frame, totally at random (and not in a cycle), for a powerful, "bubbling" jet.

✕ For a fire, we create flames of different shapes and sizes, flames we animate by replacement (see page 31), but a little less randomly than the jet of water, above. What we want to achieve are flames that steadily get bigger and smaller, but also regularly include a few chaotic moments where a few "wrong-sized" flames suddenly appear to add realism.

Lighting and Camera Special Effects

✕ We can depict lightning bolts thanks to special projectors. If you
have projectors equipped with a dimmer (if it's a professional production, this will be the case), these two animation curves work.

    —— **A big lightning bolt followed by more lightning bolts.**

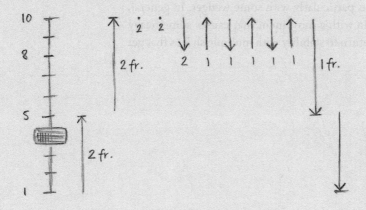

    —— **A big lightning bolt followed by small lightning bolts.**

✕ If, in addition to a physical visual effect with some kind of material (paper, aluminum, transparent plastic), you have a dimmer connected to a small localized light for the fire, vary the intensity from dim to bright and vice-versa with a maximum of four poses (two images per pose) following one direction, and, from time to time, one image in the wrong direction.

✕ Camera shake is often used to accompany a hard impact, like during a big fall, or to animate an earthquake or another kind of shaking, regardless of whether one's own point of view or not. When this effect is not used in post-production, the animator makes the camera move. It is preferable to have a tripod with pan handles, but we can get by without one, particularly with some wedges. In general, for an impact, we begin with a movement that causes some heavy misframing, then we return to stability with multiple shakes that get smaller and smaller.

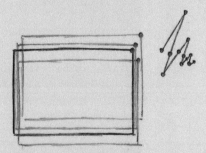

For a tremor, we increase the magnitude (i.e. the shaking from side to side), then we reduce it slowly, until everything is still.

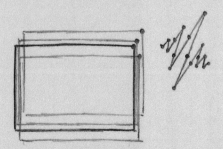

Here again, it's important to understand where the energy is coming from and where it's going. If the jolts depict a hand shaking a box, the tremors must be consistent with a movement that an arm is capable of producing naturally; if the jolts depict an impact, the spacing will be biggest right after the first image, similar to the spacing during the fall that preceded it.

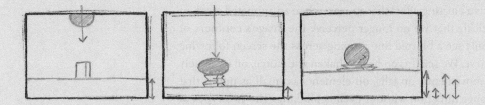

Here, the object squashes the ground on impact (this action is depicted by the camera's framing, not by a change in the ground) with a spacing similar to that of the fall, and the energy is distributed through multiple rebounds (from the camera's framing) that get weaker and weaker until the camera stops completely.

Enhanced Perception

These are probably the special effects I like the most, the ones I find the most enjoyable to make. Here, creativity really knows no bounds. All sorts of new methods can be invented.

Motion Blur

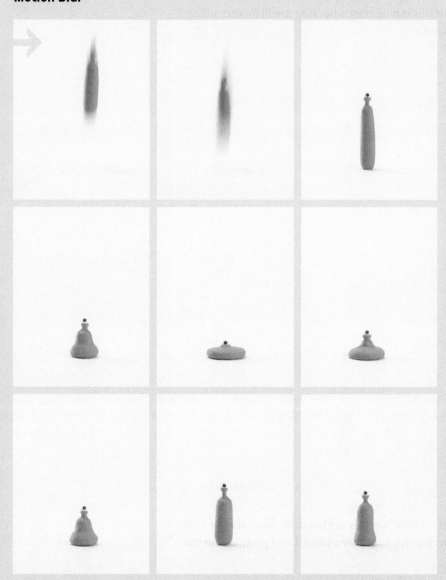

Motion blur is a blurring effect that appears when an animated element moves so quickly that we no longer perceive the image's contours or details. We only see a blurred line moving across the screen following its motion curve. We see this on heads shaken with force, on extremely fast starting movements, on falls, on elements as small as pupils that suddenly change direction without eyelids blinking. The two types of motion blur we're going to discuss are optical blur and physical blur.

× Optical blur is achieved by actually moving the element while it's in front of the camera during a take. Therefore, it is essential that the camera (nowadays, this is usually a digital single-lens reflex camera (DSLR)) has a slow enough shutter speed to allow the character or object in the image to move forward while the shutter is open. The main difficulty in creating optical blur lies in moving the element without a hand or shadow appearing in the shot. To get around this problem, we use a piece of equipment known as a rig, which helps us pull or push the object. This keeps our hand out of frame and prevents us from affecting the lighting. Nevertheless, the rig cannot appear in the blur, unless it blends in so well it can't be perceived. If this isn't the case, if the rig is visible in spite of the blurring, it needs to stay outside the blurring as much as possible. It will create its own blurred motion, but this can be erased because it will be very different from the character's.

Like this

... and not like this

× Physical blur, on the other hand, is achieved by fabricating a blur with modeling clay, paper, or another material and putting it in the object's place.

A single strip having the same color as the element can be enough to create a blurring effect. We make it so that it matches the length of the trajectory and the animated element's shape (or slightly narrower).

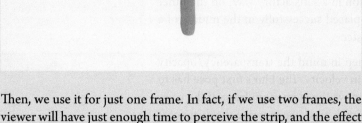

Then, we use it for just one frame. In fact, if we use two frames, the viewer will have just enough time to perceive the strip, and the effect is lost, whereas with one frame, the viewer perceives the blur without, however, seeing how it was achieved.

Sometimes, a one-colored strip isn't enough to achieve a complex, multicolor blur. If this is the case, we need to be a bit more creative and handy.

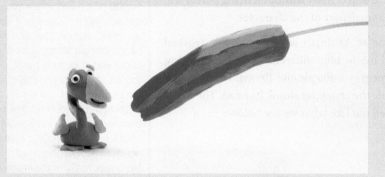

When do we use them?

We don't use blurs just whenever we feel like it. In general, we use it when the speed is too great for the eye to perceive more than a few poses (one or two) on the trajectory: for example, a rubber band we stretch out and suddenly release, an object falling from high up (coming from out of frame), a character who takes off in a cloud of smoke after anticipating an exaggerated movement (think of the coyote from the cartoon *Wile E. Coyote and the Road Runner*, mentioned on page 43).

× We aren't usually going to create a blur on a motion curve with cushioning and a change in direction, such as an object tossed in the air that slows down as it rises and, then, comes back down. In fact, the cushioning itself is an indicator that the velocity isn't fast enough for a blur to be appropriate.

× On the other hand, we can make a smear on a motion that would have a consistently repeating curve (the spinning tornado of Tax, the Tasmanian devil, for example) or on a curve without deceleration (here again, think of *Wile E. Coyote and the Road Runner* and the typical curves we see with the Road Runner when he takes off: all we see here is the dust he kicks up all along the road.

× We rarely add blur when something is already in motion and, if we do, the transition is tricky. I have never seen physical blurs added to something already in motion in a satisfactory way; on the other hand, I've seen optical blurs placed successfully in the middle of a motion that gets faster and faster.

If you want to give it a go, keep in mind the transparency/opacity rule in regards to the change in velocity. The blur's first pose has to be almost opaque: we barely move the element in front of the camera. The blurring effect is minimal. Next, we increase the distance it moves, which creates a slightly more transparent blur, then we move it a good distance, in order to achieve a lot of transparency and the impression of high speed.

× Physical blur is particularly useful when optical blur is not possible, for example when the shutter speed is too fast, when there is no way a rig can be used to move the object itself without it being perceived, or when the blur involves a small part of the character.

Richard Webber, a director at Aardman with whom I've worked on many occasions, asked me to blur different body parts during extremely dynamic movements on *Purple and Brown*. He wanted a blurry mouth and eyes while the character shook its head. The effect worked very well and turned out like what we see below:

BLUR AND OPACITY

When you create your blur, be sure to take a look where you are at in terms of opacity: if you are in mid-motion, your blur will be transparent from the start to the end of its path, but if you are at the start or end of the blur, with part of the path showing a more defined, less transparent shape, think about what kind of manipulations you will do to achieve this effect. More specifically, is the image going to capture the start or end of your gesture? Will the slightly more defined and opaque shape be situated at the start or end of the path? Will it be better to move the element in space in its real direction or in the opposite direction? If you notice that your gesture doesn't allow you to achieve the right path, try moving your shape in the opposite direction of its trajectory so you can capture the right amount of opacity, but also definition, in the right spots.

I've also had the opportunity to try adapting an effect that we can see in The Simpsons into stop-motion: the pupils, when moving to the opposite side in one single frame, resemble an hourglass. In the blurring, they get stretched out, but their shape looks a little more realistic at the beginning and end of the stretch, as if the motion started gently after the camera's shutter opened and stopped gently before it closed. This makes the change to the eyes very dynamic and makes up for the absence (by choice) of blinking eyelids (see paragraph about eyelids on page 139).

✕ Some examples

— **Example of an optical blur with a start and stop** (note here that the distance is such that we use two different blurs over two consecutive frames to cover the space traveled).

We must always signal the movement's abruptness and speed with an appropriate anticipation (see page 43).

Here, we have an anticipation over three poses, three blurred frames with different transparency levels based whether it's the start or end pose, or the middle pose (full speed), then a cushioning, a rebound, and the stop pose.

> **TAKE NOTE!**
>
> The transparency of your optical blur makes it look fast: the more transparent it is, the faster it appears to be moving; the more opaque it is, the slower.

— **Example of blur following a movement with extreme elastic tension, then a sudden loosening.** The anticipation is maintained as long as necessary (no less than three poses of two frames each), followed by a tense stop (the stop pose is shaking too) over 10-20 frames. The element under tension is then released all of a sudden. The trajectory is rendered by a straight smear blurred on one frame and, then, nothing if the element goes off screen. If the object disappears into a hole on screen, we give it back its normal shape when it enters into contact with the edge of the hole. Then, we squash it before making it fall inside the hole in its normal shape. If the object squashes on an obstacle, it does it on impact, right after the blur.

Speed lines

Speed lines are an effect that appears when the eye follows a character moving at high speed in front of a blurred scenery. They are also used in comic books and graphic novels to add dynamism to a scene when a character in the foreground is barely animated or not animated at all (think specifically of *Dragon Ball Z*).

It's almost the exact opposite of the previous effect; in fact, here, it's the scenery that appears to be moving too fast. We'll adapt this effect to stop-motion objects by experimenting with possibilities and creativity.

× If the set is light and easy enough to move, there's nothing to keep us from moving it directly (as long as the stand allowing us to shift the set is steady enough).

× Otherwise, it's also possible to take a photo of the set (as wide as the velocity is high and the distance traveled is significant), then affixing it to a steady stand that we will move behind the character (in the same way as we saw before for the character blurs, page 70).

TIP!

Once you reach a high speed and your blurred scenery is blurry enough, you can reuse the same blurry area by looping it, thus saving on the set's length.

× There is also an inexpensive solution, which consists of blurring the photo of the set with image editing software before printing it, then incorporating this blurred scenery behind the character. It might be difficult to put this scenery on paper without the viewer noticing it. Thus, it's a good idea to move the scenery right in front of the camera, in order to camouflage the paper with the help of a little more blur, which can be added to the blur already in the photo.

× Another way is by drawing, modeling or creating speed lines using cardboard (or for a bubbling effect, several pieces like with replacement animation [see page 31], in the same spirit as the physical blurs we saw previously [page 71]).

Multiples

The principle behind multiples is the same as it is for motion blur: it plays with the eye's inability to perceive an element that is moving too fast. Here, however, instead of seeing a general blur on the whole shape, we're going to let the eye perceive a part of it. We're going to stack several movements of this element's part on top of each other in one frame.

For example, if we imagine a character spinning a lettuce in a metal basket who has to spin the basket in the air extremely fast to get rid of the water, the character's arm will spin so fast the eye won't be able to follow it clearly. On the other hand, we want to provide enough details so the viewer understands the action. So, we will add a visual effect of arms repeating over the same frame ("multiple" arms). We will choose to clearly show which arm is in the real position (with the right spacing on the animation curve) and the less clear parts (less and less clear, as we get further away) of the arms immediately preceding this main position. We will then repeat this effect on the next pose, adapting the whole arm to the real pose and adding the multiple arms on the preceding poses, which we will do for the duration of the movement.

This effect is very good for movements that change direction too often for the eye to distinguish the follow-through (like a street artist who moves goblets very quickly to confuse the player and make them lose sight of the ball hidden under one of them). We will give the character a "Shiva" factor with multiple arms, each one having its own individual movement in the action overall.

EXERCISE

▶ **Your character shoots a stone with a slingshot, looks at the damage caused, and then runs away.**

Concentrate on the timing of these actions and the anticipations. Play with contrasts and the respective special effects.

See the solutions at the end of the book.

WORKING PUPPETS AND EXTERNAL SUPPORTS

This chapter deals exclusively with **STOP MOTION** animation

This chapter focuses on the logistical and technical aspects of stop motion animation. Readers who wish to explore animation without worrying about what technique to use can skip over this. Here, we're going to build a simple puppet that you can use for the exercises in this book. You can find the materials you will need in stores or online at a reasonable price. Puppets can get complex very quickly, but the purpose of this book is animation, so we won't be going into model-making in any depth.

CHOOSING A TECHNIQUE AND MATERIALS

When choosing a technique for a personal project, think about the time constraints and the reasons for your conceptual and graphical choices. If your stop motion project requires numerous deformations and transformations, you would naturally turn to modeling clay. This technique requires numerous working hours, but because it allows for almost any kind of deformation, the result will likely be just what you expected.

If you don't have a lot of deformations to do, a "hard" character covered in Milliput® (see the list of materials needed), foam, aluminum, cloth, or even paper mâché will suffice and reduce your shooting time.

When choosing materials, think about how well they keep over time and in conditions occasionally involving extreme heat. Some consumer-grade modeling clays dry out very quickly, and organic foods (vegetables, fruits, meat, etc.) change shape, e.g. rot and/or shrink, very quickly.

Here, the instructions apply to a puppet made with modeling clay.

Materials needed to make a puppet

1. Aluminum wire and copper wire
2. K&S Tubes
   (square hollow tubes that perfectly fit together)
3. Epoxy glue
4. Milliput®
   (two-part modeling putty; quick drying; can be sanded or painted after drying)
5. Adhesive cloth wrap
   (surgical tape)
6. Cotton thread
7. Quality modeling clay
   (Newplast®, Staedtler Noris Club®, Giotto Patplume®, etc.) that doesn't dry and doesn't soften too fast
8. Beads or balls
   (well rounded, unjoined for the eyes)
9. Metal square plates or round washers for the feet
10. Nuts
    (compatible with your future rigs, see page 107 and after)
11. Drill
12. Wire cutters
13. Small files for metalworking
14. Small hacksaw

Equipment needed
for the work station

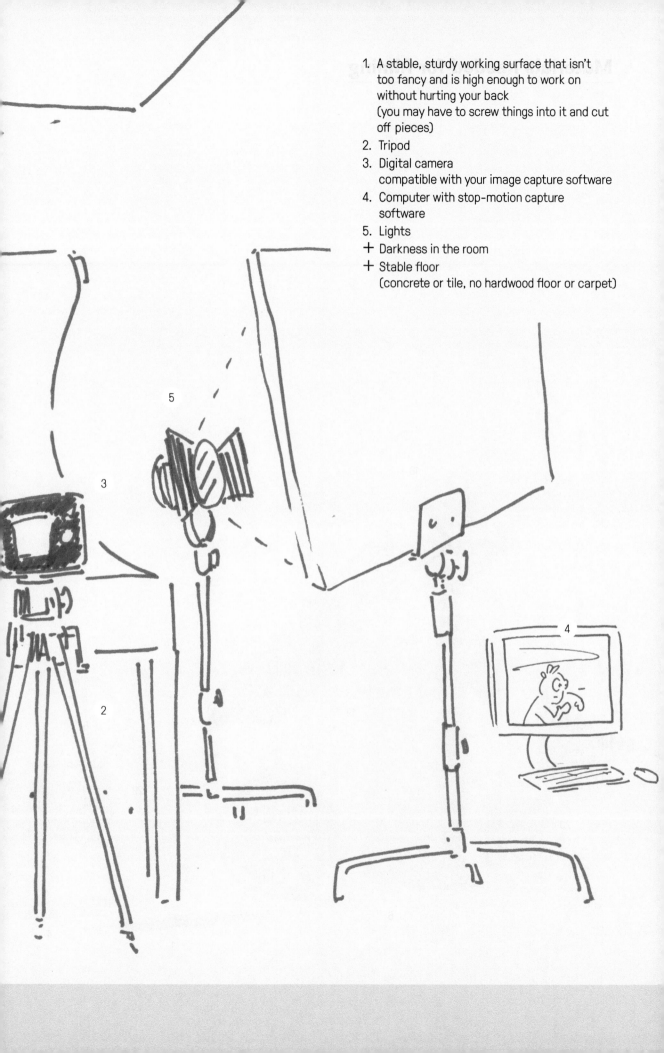

1. A stable, sturdy working surface that isn't too fancy and is high enough to work on without hurting your back
   (you may have to screw things into it and cut off pieces)
2. Tripod
3. Digital camera
   compatible with your image capture software
4. Computer with stop-motion capture software
5. Lights
+ Darkness in the room
+ Stable floor
   (concrete or tile, no hardwood floor or carpet)

Materials needed for filming

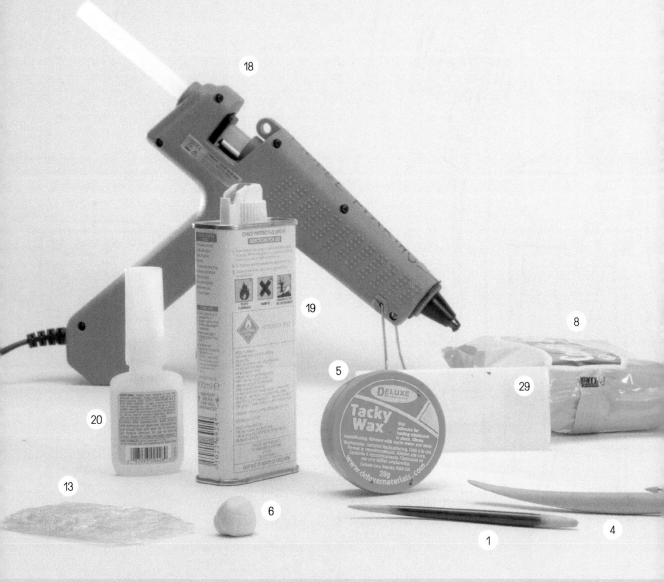

1. Handmade brush tool
   (from the wood handle of a paint brush – select your desired handle size and choose the strongest, most dense wood possible, see page 86)
2. Wire tools
   (tools for scraping and carving, see page 87)
3. Round silicone paintbrushes
   (soft – white and/or medium – gray)
4. Any other sculpting tools you may need
5. Tacky Wax®
6. Blu Tak®
7. Talcum powder
8. Hand wipes for hands and tools
9. Paper towel
10. Tooth picks
11. Cotton swabs
12. Pins
13. Plastic wrap
14. Gaffer tape
15. PTFE tape
16. Alligator clips
    (or other heavy duty clips)
17. Clamp
18. Glue gun and sticks
19. Lighter fluid
    (to easily remove hardened hot glue)
20. Super glue
21. Wire cutters
22. Scissors
23. Box cutter
24. Black permanent marker
25. Pens
26. Pencils
27. Eraser
28. White paper or notebook
29. Modeling beeswax
30. Modeling tool
to animate pupils
31. Modeling tool
(that also allows you to make eyelids)

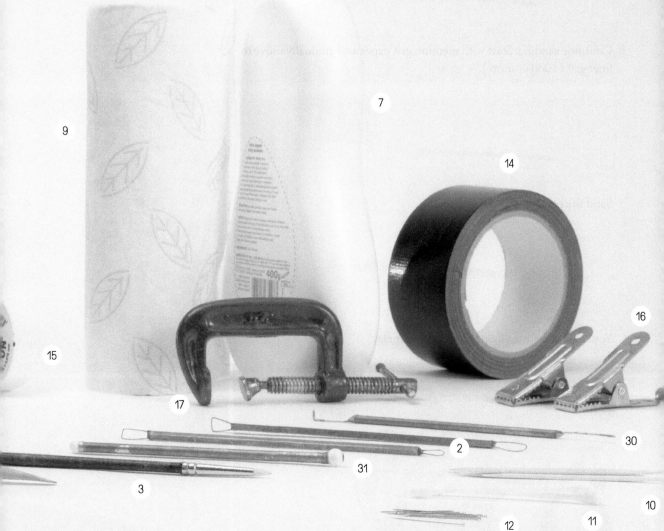

Make your own brush tool

Take a brush.

Cut off the metal part of the brush.

Sand and round the end (do not use the box cutter, it makes it difficult to smooth afterward).

Continue sanding. Start with medium grit paper and gradually move to finer grit (1000 or more).

Sand the other end into a pointed tip.

Your tool is ready to help you model your clay!

Make your own loop tool

Make your own loop tool with a hollow tube, a staple on the square end, and piano wire on the round end.

Bend the staple and shape it like in the picture so you can insert the ends into the tube. Bend the piano wire so you can insert the ends into the tube, too. Glue each of these elements to the inside of your hollow tube with epoxy glue.

You can make loop tools of any size.

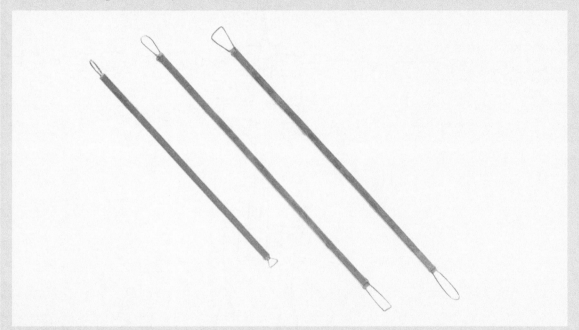

Diagram

You can make the very basic armature below right away without having to be a DIY expert. However, if you know how to solder a little, all the glued points on the square tubes can be soldered. And your armature will be even sturdier. Otherwise, not to worry: epoxy glue will be your best ally.

When designing an armature, it's important to think about what your character is going to have to do during shooting, how it will be tied down, held in the air, or fixed to some other element, whether it's going to hold or carry other elements, whether certain parts of its body will be totally hidden while others are seen up close, etc. The following diagram is good for a classic human character that will be standing most of the time.

Most often, we will need rigging points (see page 89) to affix objects in the hands and tie down the feet.

For this human puppet, the torso and pelvis are going to have a system of square tubes that easily combine with other sizes; these tubes will allow us to connect all the elements together in a precise, durable manner. Everything is then secured inside a ball of Milliput® self-hardening putty.

The limbs are made of aluminum wire twisted together – for flexible armatures – and are covered in Milliput® to reproduce the rigidity of bone. We will place a washer in the hands and feet to magnetize them later or to put a mounting bolt through them.

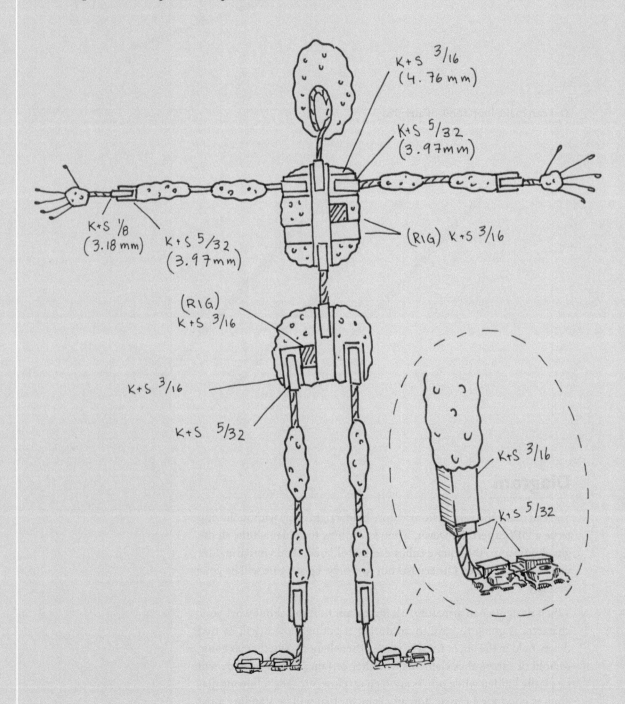

K+S 3/16
(4.76 mm)

K+S 5/32
(3.97mm)

K+S 1/8
(3.18 mm)

K+S 5/32
(3.97mm)

(RIG) K+S 3/16

(RIG)
K+S 3/16

K+S 3/16

K+S 5/32

K+S 3/16

K+S 5/32

Here are some common pitfalls to avoid when making your first armature.

✕ **Inserted lengths are too short.** The shorter your sections of K&S tubing (interlocking square tubes) are, the less precise and secure they will be. Therefore, plan to make them as long as possible.

✕ **Lack of stable, strong rigging points.** A rigging point is a point where a rig arm inserts into the character's body to hold it up externally in a stable, precise position while a picture is taken. The primary rigging point ties the feet down. However, when the character is in an unbalanced position or is completely suspended in air (for example, during a jump or fall), it has to be held at other body parts, like the side of the torso or the lower back. We must, therefore, think about where to insert these rigging points in the armature beforehand (see the different types of rigs, page 107-108 to plan your rigging points). Generally, we find rigging points on the character's seat, back, front and sides. We use a system of interlocking square tubes to ensure our puppet can be positioned accurately and stay in place.

✕ **Lack of replacements parts.** Puppets break during a shoot. It's not a question of "if" but "when." It's important to plan for possible repairs. Therefore, we're going to separate our elements and keep them independent from one another so we can replace them and repair them without having to redo the whole puppet. For example, the hands, and, more generally, any joints, break very often. For this reason, we need to devise a system that allows us to detach them from the rest of the body easily. Thus we're also going to use a system of square tubes we can insert into the extremities of the each body part. These will help us keep things separated while ensuring stability, sturdiness and precision when they are in place.

✕ **Unstable contact points.** If the feet are the contact point, instability will stem from elements that are two thin, too brittle, or covered by a complex texture that doesn't join well with the floor's surface. In animation, and especially on a tight budget or schedule, we try as hard as possible to limit the number of rigs. A character in a sitting or standing position must be stable without the external support of a rig. Its armature must, therefore, have feet (contact points) that are heavy, long and flat enough to sustain the body.

✕ **Screw threads we fail to protect from stray glue (or other) that, as a result, no longer work.** The solution is to fill the nuts or cover the screws (or threaded rods) with modeling clay before applying any substance that could run and damage them.

✕ **A puppet that is too heavy or unbalanced.** Limit the weight (particularly modeling clay which, depending on the brand, can be very heavy) by replacing a part of its bulk with hard foam (such as Plastazote®), and make sure to distribute it well so as to make the puppet lighter at the top and the extremities and heavier at the bottom.

Overall, these principles are the same no matter your character's design. For example, here's a diagram of a bird. I've decided to use the aforementioned light-weight, hard foam up top to reduce the armature's weight. Here, we can see the square tubes on the body are "plugged" (and glued) into this foam, which is going to limit the amount of modeling clay, and thus the overall weight.

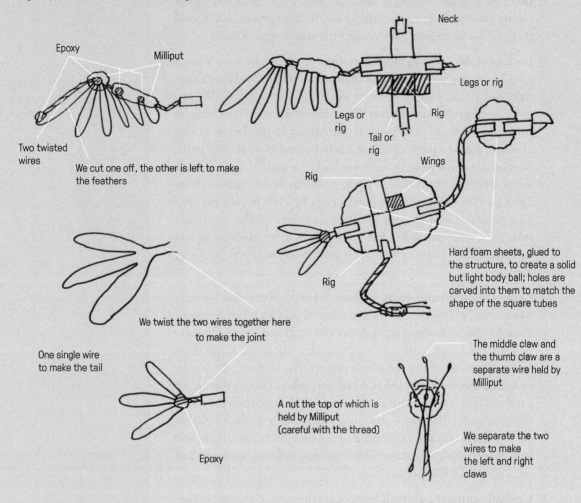

Epoxy

Milliput

Neck

Two twisted wires

Legs or rig

We cut one off, the other is left to make the feathers

Legs or rig

Rig

Tail or rig

Wings

Rig

Rig

Hard foam sheets, glued to the structure, to create a solid but light body ball; holes are carved into them to match the shape of the square tubes

One single wire to make the tail

We twist the two wires together here to make the joint

The middle claw and the thumb claw are a separate wire held by Milliput

A nut the top of which is held by Milliput (careful with the thread)

We separate the two wires to make the left and right claws

Epoxy

Puppet Fabrication Step by Step

1. Draw your diagram to scale.

2. Measure your lengths of aluminum wire. You will need two or three aluminum wires.

The number of wires depends on their thickness, the desired flexibility/stiffness ratio and the thickness of the square tubes we will have to insert them into.

Too many wires increases the elasticity, which can make the animation more difficult. Therefore, it's preferable to achieve a desired strength using a few thick wires instead of many thin wires. A set of six 1 mm diameter wires is not the same as a set of three 2 mm wires.

TIP!

You can add copper wire. In fact, copper is less breakable (but more expensive) than aluminum: if all your aluminum wires break before the end of your shoot, the leftover copper wire might give you enough strength to finish.

3. Twist your lengths of aluminum together.

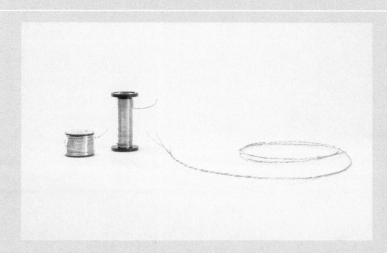

TIP!

Twist your wires together using a drill (slowly and steadily) to achieve a consistent result. It is important to not twist them too tightly together because that stretches and tenses the material, which will then be more susceptible to breakage.

4. Measure and saw pieces of square tubing to the right thickness and length.

5. File the rough edges and any residual off so the aluminum wires don't break too fast on contact.

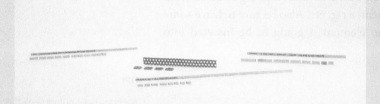

6. Glue the square tubes for the torso and pelvis together using epoxy glue.

TIP!

So that the element adheres as best as possible and stays in place, in contact with the glue, we try to give it a rough texture: crosshatching with pliers, a strip of adhesive tape glued in a loop or around the aluminum wire, chicken wire, box-cutter scoring on the surface, etc. This is also good for the modeling putty (Milliput®, or any another similar material), which could come unstuck from the element it is in contact with.

TIP!

If it looks possible, encase the elements with glue on several of their sides instead of gluing just one flat side, and apply the glue with gravity in mind (if it seems feasible).

7. With Milliput®, model the body and pelvis on the previously prepared armature.

8. Glue the lengths of aluminum wire inside square tubes with the right thickness. Make sure you know what section will be the male and which will be the female based on what is going to be inserted inside: another body element, a rig, etc. Also be sure to leave some space when the end of an element is going to be inserted into another tube.

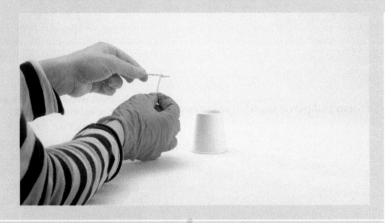

TIP!

We purposely put glue all the way to the edge, and even over it, to create a little dome around the wire, so that the rough edges of the square tubes don't prematurely sever the aluminum wire when manipulating it.

9. Make sausages with Milliput® and mold them around the sections of aluminum wire according to the diagram, then make some marks and uneven spots on the surface to help the modeling clay stick.

10. Make the feet by gluing your square tubes onto the metal plates and to the aluminum wires in the tubes. Similarly, glue a nut onto each metal plate and make sure to fill the thread with modeling clay to prevent glue from getting inside it.

TIP!

For the parts glued together but not held by Milliput®, reinforce the joints by wrapping the joined parts with cotton thread, which you will then cover in glue.

11. Make the hands by shaping the aluminum wire into a teardrop and gluing the pointed part inside the square tube. Next, place the teardrop inside a small ball of Milliput®, which you'll insert the lengths of aluminum wire into to form the fingers (while also making sure to curve the wires so they are held firmly by the putty).

TIP!

Let a small drop of epoxy glue dry on the finger tips so that the end of the aluminum wire doesn't pierce the modeling clay too easily when manipulating the puppet.

12. Form the head by twisting aluminum wires into the shape of a tear-drop. We will glue the pointed part of the teardrop inside a square tube. Next, wrap it in adhesive cloth wrap so that it sticks to the modeling clay better.

13. You armature is ready! Now it's time to use the modeling clay. Sculpt your character around your armature

For a light, thin character, opt for a simpler, less thick, less rigid armature that won't force you to press too hard on the modeling clay for every manipulation (below, on the right). This armature uses a lot less Milliput®. The feet and hands are shaped like a tear-drop. This is a supporting skeleton for the thin parts (the arms and legs, the neck), and we're counting on the modeling clay to stick to the ground well to keep the foot in place, and on the lightness of the fingers to retain their shape.

TIP!

If there is no Milliput® on a large length of twisted aluminum wire, it should be wrapped in adhesive bandage wrap so the modeling clay will adhere to it well. You can also rub beeswax on the adhesive bandage wrap and, then, model the modeling clay around it. If you don't have any beeswax, rub some modeling clay directly on it, but the results won't be quite as good.

14. If your character has very expressive eyes, a simple bead will be ideal: the bead's hole will be the pupil, and we can paint an iris around; after that, we simply move the eye using a pick/pin.

Modeling Techniques for Modeling Clay

There are many tips and tricks for modeling properly without tears or irregularities, and they are very important if we want to achieve a satisfying, professional result.

X First off, how we handle things is critical. Imagine you're handling a soft-boiled egg... without the shell. We have to maintain any volume placed in the hand and never squash anything against a surface or with our fingers. The very weight of an object placed on a table top can be enough to alter its shape. Consider using a hand wipe or a nest of paper towel to create some support.

X In addition, make sure you protect the modeling clay you are working with from dust or drying out with plastic wrap (no matter if it's been sculpted into its final shape or hasn't been sculpted yet).

X We ought to be able to click on any image and use it as a still. Even if it's an inbetween. The sculpting should be meticulous, hollowed-out areas should be black, angles and rounded areas well defined, excess clay cleaned off, and surfaces clean and consistently textured. Everything must be sculpted, crafted, and posed well so that it all comes together harmoniously.

X If you succeed at doing something once, you can do it a second time. Don't be afraid to undo something!

X In animation, we can (we must) do anything to convey our message, including pulling, pushing, transforming, adding, removing, etc. Whatever the effect is, make it happen! Sculpt, transform, and spend hours on your puppet to get the effect just right and get a big reaction from your viewer's when they see it for the first time.

Choosing the color of the modeling clay

— White and very light colors (beige, off-white) quickly pick up dust and other dirt particles in the air. Black, on the other hand, can soil other elements used in the animation. Grays and browns, or relatively dark, vivid colors that are less prone to getting dirty, are the easiest to handle.

— It is important to clean (with hand wipes) and to retexturize the modeling clay often. If you aren't filming the surface up close, it's better to begin with a character that isn't too clean. The viewer won't notice the change in color between a character that's gradually gotten dirty over a number of frames and a freshly cleaned one if we maintain an acceptable level of dirtiness from

TAKE NOTE!

Be curious about the materials at your disposal and all the possibilities they offer. For example, there are resins and plastics that can be deformed or modeled after immersing them in boiling water.

the beginning of the shot and only remove the largest dust/dirt particles.

— The colors of different modeling clays mix just like paint does. Blue and yellow will make green, white will lighten the color, etc.

— We mix colors by kneading, pulling, and folding the clay to make the marble-like look disappear and achieve a consistent color.

15. Now that you have your ball of clay in hand, the first step to modeling your puppet is to "grow" the bulk of your object's volume on the armature.

✗ When you are modeling with a uniform color, do just the opposite of what you used to do in school: avoid sticking different shapes of modeling clay together. They will invariably break off when handled at some point while shooting. If you want to minimize the risk of clay tearing or breaking off, you need to start with one ball of clay and make the parts "grow" from this one ball (for example, the arms, legs or head) instead of adding them to the body by applying additional clay. And even when you pull them off and shape them from one homogeneous piece of clay, the risk of creating tears or breakage is still high because of how much the object is handled during the animation, especially when an element is very thin (like the fingers on a hand). The need to continuously remodel your character will be unavoidable; you will, therefore, need to limit this by making sure your object is as consistent and full-bodied as possible from the very start.

✗ If you are forced to reattach an element that falls off or add one due to a difference in color, there is a technically better way of doing this. I call it the "hedgehog" technique. What you do is make a lot of small holes with a toothpick on the two surfaces you want to join together. This allows us to create well textured surfaces that will join together in a much stronger, durable manner.

✕ You can also make "stitches," if the two elements are the same color and are already touching thanks to the hedgehog technique. On the outside line where the two elements touch – i.e. the joint –, carve out two perpendicular criss-crossing furrows that are as different in size, direction and thickness as possible from one element to the other. Next, randomly put the clay back inside each element's furrows (to mix the clay as much as possible). Next, remodel and smooth out the shape.

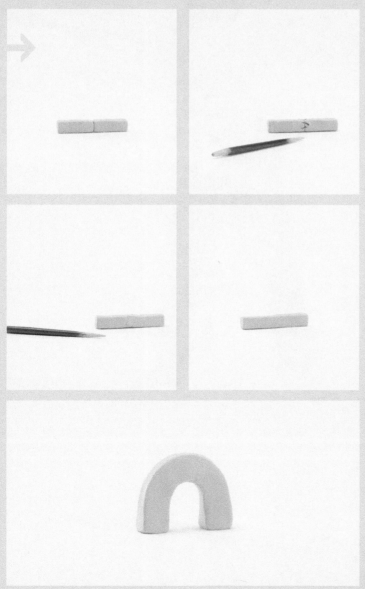

16. Push the clay into all the cracks and make it stick to your armature's entire surface.

17. Start by refining the details on your elements using your fingers and tools (your brush tool is a big help when modeling).

18. Push with the tool and roll it between your fingers (like a small pastry roller) to flatten the surface.

19. Smooth it out.

  ✕ To making smoothing easier, moisten the surface.

  ✕ As you begin to smooth the modeling clay, if several colors are next to each other, consider placing some plastic wrap over the entire area so that a color doesn't accidentally mix with another.

  ✕ While we're discussing this, keep your eye on colors that could potentially mix together while shooting (particularly colors of animated parts that are in direct contact with props). Clean things frequently.

20. Lastly, sculpt the details and add additional materials (eyes, hair, antennae, etc.)

× When modeling clay is shiny, press on it lightly – without deforming it – to put your fingerprints on it and create a matte texture.

× When a "hard" surface is shiny (a non-moldable surface like silicone or resin), pat it with some modeling clay to dull the shine.

× Conversely, if you want to make a surface shiny, apply a thin layer of colorless lubricant to each image, if the element is lively (like the tongue or eyes). If you are no longer animating the element, or if you aren't touching it too much and desire a semi-permanent result, apply clear liquid glue. For an ephemeral look or something akin to a time-lapse (evaporating water, sweat, etc.), it's better if you use hand sanitizer gel.

× When you have to add an element that is too big behind another element that you wish to keep as is, don't hesitate to cheat a little and make a small notch where you can easily insert this second element behind the first. For example, teeth biting the lower lip look as if they are no longer touching the face's surface because of the increased volume behind the teeth. By removing some modeling clay from the back of the lip, it is possible to insert the teeth into the notch we've made and reduce this part's overall thickness. This will make contact between the mouth and the face easier to achieve.

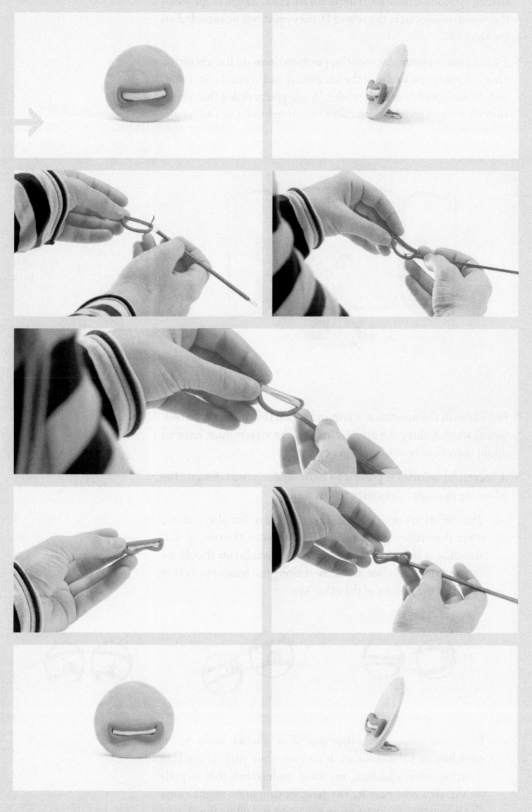

× When making a set of replacement mouths, you need to have the same amount of clay for each mouth. Therefore, you must weigh the balls of modeling clay. You can flatten the clay in a pasta machine and then cut out your shapes using a cookie cutter. You can also make a long sausage and cut pieces of the same length.

✕ If you choose a characteristic design, apply it everywhere in a consistent, systematic manner. If the teeth are cut at a right angle when the mouth pronounces the sound D, they must not be rounded on the sound K.

✕ To test your replacement mouths, position them on the character. This will allow you to check the horizontal and vertical alignment, and the consistency of each model. While you're doing this, check your character's profile by placing a mirror behind it at a 45° angle.

✕ Just like with the mouths, it is important that the thickness be consistent when making the eyelids. Indeed, the viewer must have no doubt there is only one eyelid per eye.

✕ A successful animation presents a harmonious visual design. The following examples demonstrate this well.

— The eyelids are not only pleasing to the eye but also realistic when they follow a connecting line between the two eyes. If you draw a line along the base of the eyelid, you should be able to extend this line and draw it along the base of the other eyelid, in the middle of the other eye.

— From one pose to another, the skin doesn't build up, it stretches, and the volumes don't gain, they shift. If the skin stretches over a surface, we must understand that it pulls on the elements near it. The neighboring joint might come closer together to create more elasticity and allow the skin to stretch. For example, the jaw is going to close slightly so that the mouth can make the "OO" sound.

Same for the volume: it moves from one place to another, but it does not appear or disappear. If the volume increases in one place, it decreases somewhere else (a squashing motion increases the width and reduces the height; a stretching motion reduces the width and increases the height).

— The hands are visually more interesting when we can see the third dimension. Push the thumb inward to create a curved or rounded shape. Separate the fingers, and their position and tension.

Keep in mind the real anatomy of your character. For example, the teeth are never stuck in the lip.

They go in the gums, behind the lips (even if we don't see the gums).

✕ If the modeling or picture calls for it, or if, for obvious budget reasons, you don't have all the body parts in place in each frame (for example, if the closed mouth opens slightly revealing a gap), do not forget to add some white in the mouth opening so the viewer senses the teeth are actually there behind the lips.

✕ Be curious about new materials! Sculpey® and Fimo® clay can be very useful for chewed chewing gum: in addition to having bright, vivid colors, these clays are easy to remove and do not mix with your character's clay.

✕ If the eyelids continue to detach from the eyes, put some Tacky Wax® on them or, for less residue on the eye, a thin layer of modeling beeswax.

Conversely, to keep modeling clay from sticking, especially on the eyes, apply a little talcum powder on the contact area.

Exact Reproduction

For this particular task, try to have the original model in front of you so you can handle it, feel its holes and bumps, and, above all, look at it from all angles. If this proves difficult, arrange to have as many photos as possible. The angle and the quality of the image, the lighting, and all the details are essential to making an accurate reproduction.

If you have the original model in hand, and if the material is identical and consistent (for example, a solid block of single-color modeling clay, no armature), weigh your model to determine its exact weight. If the original model contains an armature, you can subtract its weight (if you made it yourself) before you weigh it to determine how much clay you need. If the original has more than one color, you'll have to use your eye to match it in the reproduction.

After you've created the general shape (in the right size), focus your attention on a small part and work on it while comparing it to the original model from every angle. Then, move on to another small part. Use the grid pattern technique taught in school for copying a drawing. Adapt it to the shape of the object (in the illustration below, the original is a drawing, but the same technique can be applied to any original format). Concentrate on each little part before looking at the whole, before making an adjustment, before focusing on each little part again, and so on and so forth, until you achieve a satisfactory result.

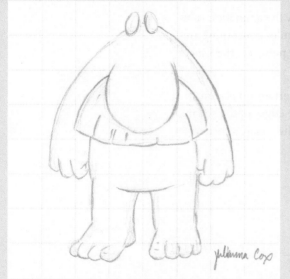 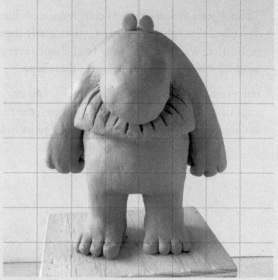

Naturally, seeing the model is very important, but touching it is essential if you have access to the original. Pass your fingertips over the original model, then yours, curve by curve, dip by dip.

When you are satisfied with the result, change the context: modify its position in the light, look at the two models in a mirror, compare and contrast them carefully and spot the differences. Observe each detail from every angle, correct differences in symmetry or size, and correct discrepancies in the sculpting.

Metamorphosis and Transformation

Animated metamorphosis is a fan favorite with modeling clay. It's not just about sculpting and modeling with precision, it's also about doing it in front of the camera, frame by frame.

If your project calls for a metamorphosis, first model the final shape (B) with a different ball of clay. Not only does this give you practice modeling shape B, you also have something to look at for reference as you work. After that, determine how much time (by number of frames) you have to go from shape A to shape B.

Lastly, think about what direction to animate in. Is shape B more complex than shape A? If so, would it be a better idea to animate in reverse order? If this is the case, you would take the time to model shape B, then a separate model A for reference that we can look at while shooting. You'll then shoot your model's metamorphosis from B to A and put your pictures in the correct order, later, during editing.

To animate a metamorphosis on screen, we follow the animation rules described throughout chapter 1, particularly the rules concerning animation curves. Visualize your final shape; every point on the object must be molded in the direction of this shape.

For example, when a circle becomes a square, certain points on the edge of circle move toward the center to form the edges of the square, while others move away from the center to form the square's corners.

The less frames you have, the faster your transformation will be and the less noticeable the errors and shortcuts will be.

The rules for increasing and decreasing energy also apply here: the faster your transformation is, the more anticipation and cushioning you will need (see pages 43-44). Begin your metamorphosis with subtle changes in phases, then gradually take things up a notch by modeling bigger and bigger changes. Once you've reached a halfway point between shape A and shape B, calmly work your way "back down" by moving from drastic changes to more subtle ones until you reach minuscule changes and an almost finished shape.

If the metamorphosis happens over a handful of frames (six or less), an anticipation in the opposite direction and a rebound may be more appropriate and dynamic. For example, you can slightly squash shape A in the opposite direction as shape B over two poses:

Then, you can model some poses in the direction of shape B:

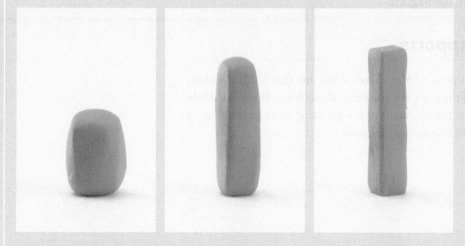

And, lastly, animate a sequence of rebounds over a few poses until the whole object is still:

SUPPORTS AND RIGS ON A BUDGET

A rig is an external support. It is there to hold the animated element in place when shooting and to keep it from being easily moved outside its animation curve (see pages 14-24) when being handled. A rig can be invisible or visible (it will have to be removed from the image digitally). It can fix the element to the set (a tied down character) or to another animated element (a piece of cloth floating in the air held by a character's hand), or it can even suspend elements in the air or hold them in an unbalanced position (a cube falling and bouncing, a character running or dancing). A rig can also replace elements of the body that are off camera. For example, if a shot is centered on a character's waistline, a rig with a winder can replace the legs and make manipulating the upper body easier. Sometimes, only the arms are on camera before going off camera. In this scenario, it is possible to remove them from the puppet's body and hold them using a rig off camera.

Rigs are essential in stop motion animation. It is impossible to make a quality film without fixing and stabilizing everything. We must think about how we design our rigs and keep them in mind when working on all the other elements for the film: sets, armatures, accessories, placement, camera angle, lighting, etc.

Ground Supports

The rig most often used on film shoots is the one that holds the character on the set. If the puppet's armature allows for it, the most stable solution is to screw the character to the set using a nut in the rigging point. This is what's known as a tie-down.

Otherwise, several options are possible...

✕ If you placed a metal washer on the soles of the armature's feet, you can hold your character down with magnets. For this to work, however, the set has to be quite thin, or made of metal. The magnets must also adapt to heavy loads: not only must they be capable of magnetizing the metal washer through the set, but they must also be able to hold the character in an unbalanced position. This technique poses the risk of losing your character's position, or the risk of it falling, if the magnet is not powerful enough to support the weight or strong enough for you to manipulate the character. A lot of animators prefer the stability and sturdiness of tie-downs, while many others prefer the speed of placement and minimal disruption that magnets offer.

✗ You can also glue the soles of your character's feet down with hot glue. The results can vary, though, and accidents can happen. In some scenarios, you may need to remove the hot glue, which you can do by applying a few drops of lighter fluid to the surface in question and carefully removing the glue.

✗ Below is another extremely simple system that doesn't require any particular equipment: tie the character down with aluminum or copper wire. First, pass the wire through a small hole made in the set, then over the foot, and lastly through another hole in the set. Next, twist the wire to tie the foot down (the leg, the pelvis, or another part of the body), and, to finish, remodel the shape of the foot to camouflage it.

ATTENTION!

Naturally, it would be tempting to insert a magnet directly in the character's feet, but this false good idea would quickly become a nightmare. Indeed, as soon as the foot would come near the ground, though without touching it, the magnet would try to stick to it and make manipulation very complicated.

✕ You can also use Blu Tak®, but the results aren't very encouraging, and using this material isn't recommended for animated characters or elements that may frequently be brushed by your hands while manipulating. Blu Tak® is actually too elastic for animation and does not resolve problems involving instability or a lack of sturdiness. It is really only recommended to hold elements far away from the working area that are stable on their own and just need to be stable for the duration of the shot.

✕ Even for this task, Tacky Wax® is the go-to material. In fact, it isn't as thick between the element and surface as Blu Tak® is, and it temporarily fixes the elements more firmly. In addition, it doesn't leave much residue on non-porous surfaces (the residue is easy to remove with a hand wipe or damp cloth).

Aerial Supports

Aerial supports are more complex because they must support a part or all of the off-balanced or flying element's weight. There is a wide array of rigs for professionals and hobbyists for sale online. Here, I'm going to talk to you about less expensive ones, i.e. homemade rigs.

An aerial support consists of a sturdy base, a flexible yet stable arm, and a plug you can insert in the animated element.

✕ **The flexible arm can be made in different ways.**

— This can be made from an aluminum wire thick enough to support the weight, or several strands twisted together for increased strength. The heavier and further from the base the element is, the stronger the arm needs to be. Aluminum wire is not very precise: we have to move it farther than necessary for the recoil effect to bring it back to the right position. In addition, the farther from the base the element is (i.e. the longer the aluminum wire is), the greater the recoil effect.

— We can make a somewhat more stable articulated arm and eliminate the aluminum wire's recoil effect by inserting small strands of wire into the tubes, or by modeling Milliput® sausages around the wire along the arm.

— We can also make the support from fishing line. We can suspend an element from above, but we can also hold it from the
side by connecting a wire between an object off camera and the
object's point of instability.

× **The rig's base can also come in different forms.**

— It can simply be hot glue or a screw fixing the end of the wire to
the floor (or another sturdy surface).

— It can also be a heavy, stable base that acts as a counterweight
to the element held in the air – for example, a flat paperweight
or scale weight – that we'll attach the aluminum wire to (using
screws, epoxy glue, an electrical block epoxied or screwed into
place into which we can insert the tip of the flexible arm, etc.)

— If we build our set on a metal set to move the character's feet
with magnets, we can use one of the magnets as a sturdy base
(Since it is held sturdily to the stage floor) and glue an electrical
block to it (as before).

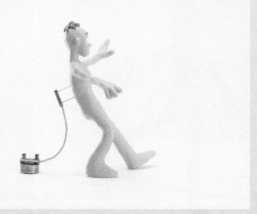

× **The insertable plug can also vary.**

— The sturdiest kind of insertable plug will be a small length of
square tubing that will fit into matching sockets on your armature's rigging points; this will be glued to the end of the flexible
arm.

— Otherwise, a simple or complex system of pins inserted into the modeling clay may be enough if the character's or element's weight is light enough. We can glue a pin or two right onto the end of the arm. It is also possible to place a row of pins along a tube that we put aluminum wire into. Here, the advantage using a row of pins is greater stability. The character can be easily turned around if it's only poked with one pin. With two or more pins, the pose is stable and remains as it should.

✕ If the character's weight is too heavy to be held in the air, in some instances we can help hold the element in the air for just enough time to get the shot. To do so, we'll use some ultra-discreet holders to avoid having to remove them digitally, later.

—— We can use very straight rod-like items, such as fine pins (entomology pins are likely the thinnest), piano wire, which is both thin and hard to bend, etc. By painting them with black matte paint, we can reduce how visible they are in the shot.

—— It's also possible to use small pieces of plexiglass, varying in length, that we can cut from a totally clear plexiglass rod. The best choice is a square-shaped rod. We orient one side of the rod toward the camera so that it's as invisible as possible. If the plexiglass rod is round, it will give off too many reflections and be very visible in the shot.

Fixing an Element to Another Animated Element

It can be complicated to fix an element to another when the second element is also being animated (for example, fixing one character to another, such as cowboy on a horse). Because the support is also changing poses from frame to frame, consequently it isn't stable or sturdy.

✗ If the joint doesn't have to hold up too much weight, or if it doesn't have to support numerous movements, many of the solutions covered in the preceding paragraphs can be applied here. We can use:

—— pins;

—— Blu Tak®, if the elements are hard;

—— Tacky Wax®, even for modeling clay;

—— fishing line, which we tie around the elements, cover with modeling clay and then remodel;

—— glue, if we want it to be permanent.

✗ If the elements are too heavy or too animated for these kinds of connections, we'll use the rigging points incorporated in our character's armatures.

—— Using the small lengths of square tubing connected to aluminum wire, we can join two elements together.

—— If an element doesn't have a rigging point on it (for example, an accessory with no armature), we can make a hole big enough to insert and glue a socket in it, where we'll insert the end of a connecting tube.

WATCH OUT!

You have to be wary of fast-drying super glue. Indeed, what it sticks to best are your fingers! When we have super glue on our hands, modeling and, in particular, texturing a surface made of modeling clay become virtually impossible. There is only one thing you can do: grab a piece of fine-grit sandpaper and rub until you can find your fingers under the glue.

Moreover, small drops of super glue on a character, an accessory or on a scenery element are permanent. Even if you unstick a drop, it leaves behind residue (as opposed to hot glue, the residue of which we can remove with lighter fluid). Nevertheless, super glue is appropriate in certain scenarios. Indeed, it works with modeling clay rather well. If it comes unglued, it will most likely be a tear right on the glue joint. Thus, we can attach small, light accessories in a character's hands if we're only going to use them for one shot. After that, we can remodel the hands for the following shots. Super glue also sticks really well to silicone. If the silicone is solid enough, we can expect the super glue to hold permanently, which means we won't be able to use the elements again without residual damage. In contrast, super glue does not stick well to plastic and many other materials at all, contrary to popular belief.

— Sometimes, a hole just big enough to fit the aluminum wire can be enough to hold the accessory in place.

— For a hard, very heavy element (resin, wood, etc.) with no rigging point on it, it is possible to make a sturdy, semi-permanent rigging point by screwing an electrical block on it in a hidden area. The center area on the electrical block is where a small screw will attach the block to the surface, and we will run an aluminum wire from the electrical block's tubes and connect it to the other animated element.

Internal supports

Often, the need to animate a soft accessory forces us to create an internal support, which will be built into the object itself.

✕ For example, we'll place a thick, strong sheet of aluminum foil between two layers of cloth (or any other flat, soft surface) glued together (in the photo, the aluminum foil is matte black).

✕ We can also place an aluminum wire around the perimeter and run it in an S-shape or spiral on the inside, between the two layers of cloth.

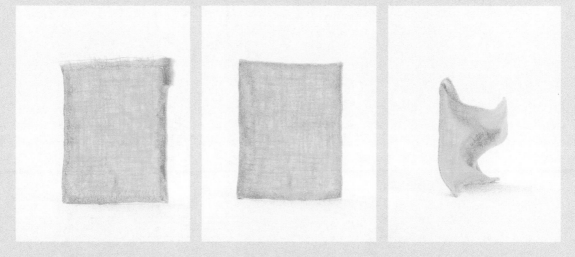

✕ To animate a rope (or a string), all we have to do is cover a thick aluminum wire in glue and, then, twist it together with the rope (or the string).

✕ Sometimes, for a rope moving in response to another animated element moving rather slowly, or when the rope is tensed, it is preferable to have real rope without aluminum wire hidden inside so we can achieve a perfect curve (or straightness).

Additional tips when using rigs

✕ Watch out for shadows! If a rig is placed in the character's shadow (or in front of it), we'll have just as much trouble in post-production as if the rig had been placed in front of the animated element. If we can't avoid this, we'll need to take an empty picture – without the rig but with the shadow in place – so we can clean the image in post-production.

✕ The more joints a rig has, the less strong it is: the leverage is greater and the number of joints to tighten is higher (if it's a professional ball and socket rig). On the other hand, the more joints a rig has, the less it impacts the character's overall pose.

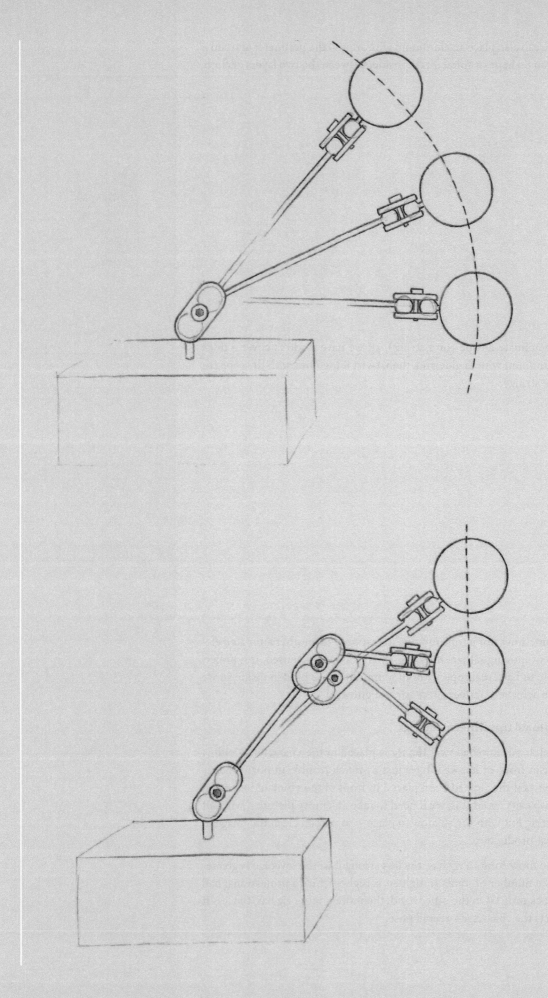

On the opposite page, a single straight arm generates a curved movement for each height change, whereas incorporating an arm with a joint in the middle allows us to compensate and change the animated element's height without affecting the animation curve.

✕ Tip: hot glue can generate long strands invisible to the naked eye that float lightly on screen like a spiderweb. They will occasionally catch light and flicker on screen. If this happens, consider melting the strands by placing the tip of the glue gun as close as possible to the glue blob.

✕ Hide rigging points or holes with modeling clay of the same color, same for hard accessories or scenery elements.

✕ Do what you can to get along well with the post-production team (and the producers). Your colleagues are going to have to erase your rigs using software and, as talented as they are, they can't always work miracles. They need to have a photo of what is behind the rig in their possession so that the rig can be replaced in the scene by the "empty" part of the image (with the same framing, the same lighting, and same focal point). They must also cut around your character on any points touching the rig. To make their job easier or to avoid having to shoot the scene again, keep in mind the following tips.

— Always try to hide your rigs behind your animated element or scenery elements.

— If they aren't hidden, try to reduce the visible area (where the rig is touching the animated element) as much as possible.

— Never leave your rigs in front of an animated element.

— If there is no other way, take a picture of the element that is behind the rig, but without the foreground element and its rig so the post-production team has the clean element behind your rig.

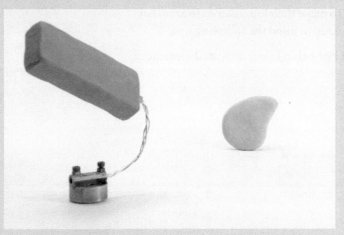

— Think about the shadows cast on the animated elements by the rig. In the illustration below, the rig is not in front of any moving elements, which is very good. However, it's casting a shadow on the blue element; the post-production team will have to remove it as if it were the rig itself, by recreating the elements's color and texture, since there is no "empty" image (an image with no rig or shadow).

—— Also avoid placing rigs in front of any animated elements' shadows. In fact, if this happens, the post-production team won't have to totally "repaint" the element behind it, they'll have to "repaint" its shadow, which may be even harder.

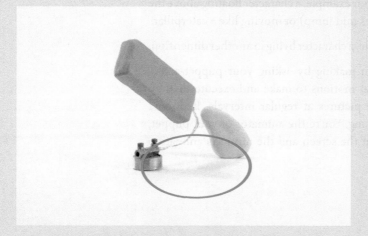

—— Just as we need to take a picture without the rig if a rig is going to be in front of an animated element, we also need to take a picture without the rig – and just with the animation's shadow – if the rig is going to be in front of an element's shadow.

PIXILATION: STOP MOTION WITH A LIVING PUPPET

Pixilation is probably the easiest way into animation, and more specifically stop motion. In pixilation, we animate human beings as if we would with puppets.

The actor moves from frame to frame according to the animator's instructions and holds a pose in each frame.

Naturally, there is no need to make a puppet, here. In fact, the puppet at our disposal is already sturdy, well designed and has joints that work perfectly! Pixilation also allows us to really feel the spacing and timing, and that's why it's a perfect introduction to the concept of the animation curve (see pages 14-24).

Certain considerations are specific to this technique and are worth listing here.

✕ The camera's exposure time must be set to a minimum to limit blur, which is inevitable with a human body. Indeed, the human body is unstable and is subject to continuous, minuscule movements. Try to think of a way to make the body a little more stable. For example, by having the actor lean against a wall or something sturdy in the scenery, or prioritizing stable poses (feet in a diagonal fashion, one foot forward, one back, rather than feet together).

✕ It is important to respect the actors by choosing poses and movements their muscles can bear and by giving them regular breaks.

When writing your scenes, then, opt for very short shots.

What makes pixilation really interesting is what it offers compared to film making and live-action shots.

✕ An instant comical effect. For example, a character floating above the floor (we only take pictures mid-jump) or moving like a caterpillar.

✕ A surreal effect. For example, a character living in another dimension.

Don't try to do "classic" film making by asking your puppet-actors to decide for themselves what motions to make and execute them in slow-motion while you take pictures at regular intervals. It doesn't bring you or teach you anything. You're the animator of your puppet, and you're the one looking at the screen and the motion's animation curves.

EXERCISES

▶ **To get familiar with straight-ahead animation,
animate a bird in flight with your own hand.**

Getting the right shape of the wings in flight is not a priority here.
What's important is to concentrate on the timing and the motion in the air.

▶ **Experiment with the concepts of speed and dynamism.**

Place an object on a table, then animate your hand reaching out and grabbing it. Do the same thing again, but this time snatch it away.

Share your creations on social media with **#SecretsoftheAnimator**

ANIMATION OF HUMAN CHARACTERS

Human character animation is without
a doubt the most important to master. To
trigger emotions in the viewer and draw
them into the story, it is absolutely
essential to appeal to their empathy.
We must, therefore, imagine a character
who answers to the same physical
and intellectual laws as the viewer, in
other words human laws, even when
the animated character is not human
(animal, object, monster, etc.). Getting
the viewer to identify with the character
is absolutely essential, but it can be
achieved in many ways. The viewer tends
to directly identify with a character (the
hero, generally) when they see themselves
positively reflected in that character;
however, the viewer can also identify
with a character when they recognize
a personality from their surrounding, or
cultural environment (generally, the
antagonizing or secondary characters).

The animator is the actor in an animation film, except that the acting is by proxy because the animator doesn't produce the motions with their own body. Instead, the animator cobbles the motions together using an external object: the animated character. Animators must, therefore, put themselves in their character's shoes (in the same mindset, in the same context) and make the character respond like they, themselves, would (same timing, same motions, etc.). This work requires exceptional observational and analytical skills, but also the ability to depict motions as accurately as possible, which makes this an extremely exciting role to be in.

And that's not including all the other motions that actors themselves aren't responsible for (for example, an actor instinctively putting on a coat; the animator has to know how to break down and recreate this action exactly), the physical movements to a multitude of objects and special effects (a glass falls and breaks naturally when we film it live, but this same action becomes very complex in animation), and, ultimately, the fact that in straight-ahead animation (in stop-motion or other frame-by-frame techniques), the animator "plays" all the characters in a scene at the same time.

GENERAL BUT ESSENTIAL ADVICE ABOUT ACTING

Acting

A convincing performance is mainly the fruit of great confidence in one's self and in the character's actual reactions. Don't be afraid of your convictions. Do what you think is right! Go all in on your decisions and follow through on your choices. If you can't totally commit, if you hesitate, if something seems off or odd, if you don't understand certain actions or reactions, discuss it in detail with the director to better understand the character's personality. You need to make the character someone unique, you have to understand and become the character.

Whichever personality you decide on, make sure you and the director agree on something uniform, logical and consistent. If the character has a crazy, absurd attitude, the animator must work within the same crazy logic, within the same kind of inner chaos.

Get the character in your head and "in your hand" a little beforehand by sculpting some poses, by experimenting with attitudes, or by sketching different stances. Bring the character's personality out physically, make it tangible.

Never forget your main subject, the message you're trying to convey. Condense it into one or two key words you can keep in mind when considering each movement, each pose, each scene.

Make a plan! Everything must be planned and written down on your exposure sheet. This can completely change your preparation prior to shooting. For example, if you need your character to open its eyes wide with showing as much white as possible in their eyes, make sure that the eyelids and eyebrows go down lower over your eyes beforehand; this will allow you to contrast this extreme pose at the desired time. Another example: if a tear is supposed to run down your character's cheek, make it appear just above the lower eyelid, then get bigger until it gets too big and runs down the cheek in the desired frame. In order to be credible, this action requires time and we need to set it up well in advance.

Simplicity and Clarity

Actions should only be present (i.e. animated) if there is a reason for them, no matter that reason (conveying an emotion, unconscious body language revealing an inner conflict, physical fatigue, a conscious yet dissimulated emotion, etc.). An animator must never animate actions because they are bored, nervous, lost confidence in the timing, or have the impression they should fill in moments of inaction. Indeed, when a character is "over-animated," the meaningful actions get lost in all the filler.

Not everything has to be moving all the time. Don't muddle your animation with small, useless secondary animations (one common mistake, for example, consists of over-animating the eyebrows).

On the other hand, when we want to show frantic brain activity, keeping the character in constant motion can help convey the message. This can also be as subtle as a trembling eyelid or a nervously tapping foot.

Identify key moments in the speech and accompany them with appropriate facial expressions and body poses.

Sometimes, as the saying goes, less is more. Anger can be more effective when it is barely contained (a still, tense body) than when it's really explosive.

Timing

It is essential to give your character time to react and the viewer time to read the action.

✘ Reaction time

The character has to have a realistic reaction time to be credible, but the viewer also needs time to analyze the action. The reaction times below are a guide to help you determine the right pacing and duration for your actions throughout your animation.

— **Under 6 frames:** no reaction.

— **6-12 frames:** reflex reaction that doesn't pass through the brain (for example, closing our eyes when something is about to hit us in the face).

— **12-24 frames:** learned reflex reaction that passes through the brain (for example, braking in front of an obstacle).

— **Over 24 frames:** reasoned reaction. Let's take a conversation, for example: we think before reacting. If we react faster, it's because we've anticipated what's being said based on the first few words, or, the opposite, because we were shocked: our surprise is a reflex, which has a reaction time of around 12 frames.

Experience can lead you to make other choices on a case-by-case basis, but while you're learning the ropes, it is highly recommended you stick to these durations. Reaction times that are too short are an

There is no need for the speech to be accompanied by gestures that visually reproduce to a tee what the viewer is perfectly capable of hearing. Expressive body communication that is totally synchronized with speech is typical of classical theater actors or silent films. For example: "I hear the king's soldiers coming." The character's exaggerated attitude is nothing more than a completely useless repetition of the line of text.

The gestures and body language are more interesting when they are out of sync with the speech. Below, we have the same line of text ("I hear the king's soldiers coming."), but the character is moving in the other direction

The acting is also more interesting when it shows something that isn't being said. In the third example, still with the same text "I hear the king's soldiers coming," the character is clearly hearing what's being said, but his expression reflects what's going on in his mind, and it doesn't bode well at all.

all-too-common mistake.

Here, too, be brave! If a character doesn't do anything for 1, 3 or even 7 seconds, it has to remain still for a while, leave it be.

It is better to have a few sustained big/meaningful poses than a long sequence of poses that drown each other out.

However, this doesn't mean that meaningful poses should be totally still. We can leave a secondary character or element completely motionless for a while, but in a quality animation, the main element, the one the viewer focuses their attention on, must be animated even when it's not in motion. What's important is that we get the sense that the character is alive. Therefore, we have to animate these big poses just enough to keep them alive, while at the same time giving the viewer time to read and analyze the situation.

Don't be afraid to lose a big pose either. Give the viewer time to see it, but don't remain on a great pose if your character loses all life while suspended in time. Simply concentrate on another big pose by changing the angles and movements of the body.

✖ The illusion of animation time

One of the most common inner conflicts with animators, particularly in stop-motion animation, is the difference between animation time (the time spent animating a motion, i.e. a time that can be very long) and real time (the time the motion lasts on screen, i.e. a time that is generally very short).

Animators can be easily influenced by the animation time. They often tend to think of the number of frames as the number of seconds. Six frames can actually seem as long as six seconds and, therefore, long enough to stop an action and start another. But six frames (which can be long in animation time, in other words working time) represent but a quarter of a second in real time, which is certainly not enough time for an entire action.

Therefore, it is critical to regularly convert the number of frames into fractions of a second and to stay (relatively) firm on the timing decided on during preproduction, when the ideas were all very clear and when we weren't in the middle of animating the same pose for four hours straight.

Give any actions and expressions enough time to settle in and take place. Ideally, we should be able to stopwatch an action and divide the time into the number of poses, but some motions are too fast to do this easily. One thing you can do is film yourself and analyze the time of the actions frame by frame. Watch and evaluate what you're animating, using the video as feedback. When in doubt, never hesitate to do an extra pose (it can be almost imperceptible), since we rarely ever slow an action too much. If, however, this last pose weakens the action, if it saps the movement's dynamism and energy, we can bring our character back to the preceding pose and stop there. Just the opposite, it is often harder to correct a motion stopped too abruptly.

TIP!

Make a still pose come to life (from the trickiest, most complex to the simplest):

– animate the character ever so slightly on one side for roughly ten frames (or more) to give it a subtle, natural swaying motion (each motion should be barely perceptible to the eye), then a handful of frames after in the other direction;

– animate other surrounding elements;

– rub the eyes with a wet finger to change their brightness;

– lightly touch the surface with your fingers to change the texture of the skin, hair or clothing;

– lock the character's eyes onto multiple spots (watch out, this always indicates a thinking process or an intense inner life);

– add a blink.

INTERESTING FACT!

The human brain reads a word faster than it recognizes a face.

Asymmetry

Much like desynchronization, which helps us bring a form of harmony to our animation based on physical reality (see pages 36-40), asymmetry also makes poses more harmonious and pleasing to the eye, and is also based on physical reality. Indeed, the body is almost always in an asymmetrical position, just like the face, which moves asymmetrically either because it is purposeful (consciously or subconsciously),

or because years of asymmetrical movements have shaped the muscles differently and the muscles no longer react in the same way.

Try going from one pose to another with dynamic, asymmetrical lines, and avoid vertical or horizontal lines, which are basic and uninteresting.

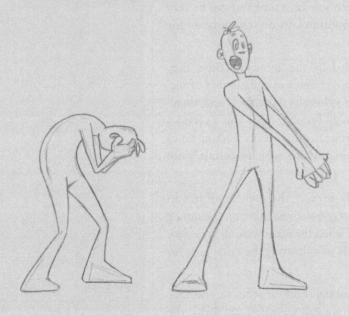

Let's take a moment to stop and consider the elements of the face, which are undoubtedly a main means of communication. Here, we're going to take a look at each part of the face and discuss each teaching point in detail, one by one.

The Eyes – The Look

The viewer generally locks their eyes onto the main character's eyes. The eyes might quickly move off the character to read an important element in the scene and analyze it when it needs to be seen directly, then the eyes will immediately lock back onto the main character's eyes. The rest of the scene is analyzed by peripheral vision and quick glances.

It is, therefore, imperative that the animator be very accurate with the eye animation at all times during their work.

✘ Eye mechanics

The eyes must be regarded as two distinct elements that influence each other. They are connected by an invisible string. It's the eyes' mechanics that always makes them move together in the same direction. They are completely connected to each other: the pupils have to move with the same timing, in the same direction, and have the same spacing.

This rule always applies, except when we want to use the eyes to depict a mental or motor skill problem (cross-eyedness, a twitchy eye, an eye that wanders, then refocuses), or show, in a very subtle animation, two dreaming, unfocused eyes in the process of refocusing on the action (the opposite is possible too, even if it is extremely complicated to depict two focused eyes starting to dream on screen).

The eyes are the only part of the body that move like a bird, with very little or no inbetweens, and no rebound effect.

When they are small on the screen, or the distance covered by the pupils is short, they can be animated without any inbetweens.

In a close-up (or extreme close-up), or when the distance is long, we need to give the motion more inbetweens: at least one cushioning frame extremely close to the final pose (which can be just a third of the size of the pupil!) and one ramping-up frame.

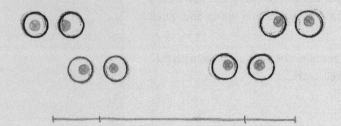

This only applies to the eyes! The rest of the body, even the tiniest part (like the eyelid, albeit closely associated with the eye), reacts according to normal muscle physics, which means that every motion is anticipated and initiated by an energy source, progresses through a normal animation curve in a more or less dynamic fashion, and ends with a cushioning and a minimum amount of inertia (smoothly or suddenly, but a cushioning nonetheless, with or without a rebound).

TAKE NOTE!

In cartoon-style animation, we very often employ a very unrealistic dynamism for the eyelids: they are completely shut for two frames, then completely open with no inbetween. This particular treatment accentuates the comic effect.

✖ **What is a focused look?**

A focused look is a look where the eyes cross slightly when looking at an object. An unfocused look is a look where the eyes do not cross at all: they are perfectly parallel with each other.

The exact distance between the pupils provides a lot of information: if the object of attention is close, we must put the pupils closer together (cross the character's eyes) to show that the distance is short; if the object is far away, we separate the pupils. As we saw in the previous paragraph, when a character isn't looking at anything (daydreaming), the pupils are totally parallel.

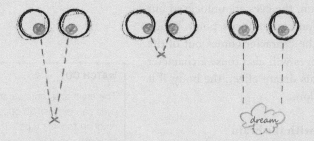

The eye direction is extremely important. When we set the eyes on a direction for the first time, we must constantly come back to the first image in order to reset them correctly when they look in this same direction again.

To set the eyes, we proceed as follows:

— we set each eye independently in the desired direction (if necessary, we hide one eye so it doesn't influence us on the other);

— next, we make sure both eyes are looking in the right direction;

— lastly, we check with the preceding frame(s) to make sure they are moving together in the same direction and have the correct distance between them.

To bring the quality up a notch, consider adjusting the look ever so slightly after a drastic change in direction. Here, we'll imagine that the character is looking in the direction of a specific point for the first time. He's just looking around, and out of the corner of his eye he sees an object. His eyes (and often his head) turn in that direction locking onto a point somewhere (with some subtle cushioning). Then, about four frames later, he focuses on the object itself just above, below or next to the initial point of focus. This effect makes the sequence of looks more realistic.

The eyes are always focused on a specific point. When we turn the head, they lock onto a point, then another, etc. throughout the rotation, at a rate of four to six frames per point, minimum. They do not turn in sync with the head.

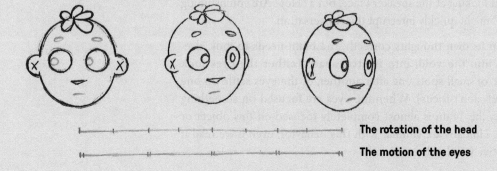

The rotation of the head

The motion of the eyes

As we saw before, during a daydream, the eyes are unfocused but locked onto a specific, albeit vague and out of focus, point. When the eyes lock onto another point, the character comes out of the daydream. Similarly, a blink of the eyes will also rouse a character from its thoughts. To accentuate this dream effect, the body, if it must move, will move in slow motion.

✖ The eyes are in direct contact with the brain

The brain thinks something, and the eyes express the thought an instant before it is put into words.

To make a character more lively and depict an inner thought bubbling up, lock the eyes onto different points over a number of frames (8, 10 or 16, at random...but no less than 6). When the character knows what it's going to say, it locks its eyes a little longer and, then, comes back to the scene's main anchor point (this may be another character or the object of the thought).

WATCH OUT

The brain and therefore the eyes can express an opposite emotion to what a person is saying.

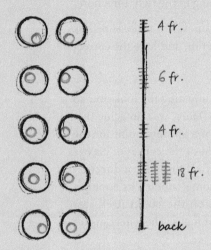

Observe a conversation in everyday life: what elements are indicative of attentive, concerned, focused or caring listening? Most of the time, the person listening looks at the person who is speaking in the eyes. Someone who doesn't look at the speaking person in the eyes, someone who's looking at something else, or nothing at all, is going to generate a little tension in the person speaking, who will feel they aren't being listened to. A person who looks "disconnected" is perfectly capable of understanding the words without looking at the speaker's face, but a "Hey! Are you listening to me?" might quickly interrupt the conversation.

To form its own thoughts correctly, the brain needs to look elsewhere, into the void, into neutral space (either the eyes look at a lot of small spots one after another, or the eyes settle on one spot but don't focus). When the eyes are focused on something specific, the brain is almost completely focused on this object or person. Humans are familiar with this behavior, even if we read it instinctively and subconsciously.

The animator is going to use these tools. When our character gets ready to speak or thinks about what to say, it looks off to the side into the void, and then says what it has to say with just a few quick looks at the other character to check that they are listening and understand. When our character is done, or if our character gets interrupted, it immediately turns its attention back to the other character and listens (and looks) intently, until its own thoughts cause them to look elsewhere.

It so happens that there are times when we observe someone who looks another person straight in the eyes while talking. This behavior shows that the person in question knows exactly, i.e. by heart, what they are going to say. They do not need to think about it at the same time.

On the other hand, a person who completely closes their eyes while talking is showing that their brain is totally incapable of thinking and communicating coherently should the slightest visual stimulus come and interfere with their thoughts.

A well-devised head/look desynchronization can help you convey subtle emotions just right. For example:

— Turning a character's head in mid-thought, while their eyes remain fixed on the previous spot, highlights the intensity of the inner thought. A distraction arises, but the character doesn't want to be distracted because it hasn't completed its thought yet. Here, a blink of the eyes will generate the change in look.

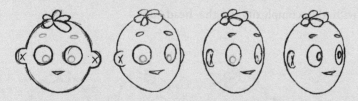

— Here, it's the opposite: we keep the head still where it is and move the eyes in the direction of the distraction. The objective is to show the character getting very bored – in spite of its efforts to concentrate – and its mind doing its best to entertain itself.

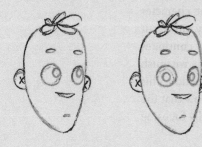

— In the same vein, to express nervousness, confusion, insinuation or disagreement, the eyes remain locked on the same spot while the head is already turning. After that, the eyes catch up with the head, but there is no blink during this transition. And when the eyes settle on the new focal point, we will add a neutral blink.

— During a shock or surprise, the eyes move before the head, whereas the blink is delayed. This shows that the surprise is so big that the character doesn't have the time to move its body (its head): the character looks at the source of the shock before anything else.

You can also experiment with the complexity of the head/look desynchronization.

To depict hesitation, confusion, or inner conflict when a character is following a conversation, we can animate a head motion in phases and accompany it with desynchronized looks. The character will turn its head in the direction it is looking, then, very quickly, it will look at the character that is speaking while its head continues to move. Lastly, we will reunite the head and the look: as we finish the head motion, the look moves with it in the same direction. This slight, temporary desynchronization will be enough to show that the character is checking it got the right impression before fully focusing its attention on someone else.

✕ Some examples of meaningful looks

— The look toward the sky, common to a non-verbal disagreement, follows the sequence below:

1. The eyes, in the middle, look ahead.

2. We place the start of a blink with the eyelids slightly lowered and the eyes unlocking from their anchor point.

3. The blink is complete; the eyelids are closed.

4. As the eyelids open, the eyes begin to roll to the side (for example, they're looking down to the left).

5. Next, when the eyelids are open more, we have another pose into the rolling (to the side).

6. The eyelids are completely open; the eyes are looking upward (here, up to the left)

7. After a minimum six-frame stop on this high point, we make another blink pose with the eyes looking downward again and the eyelids almost closed.

8. The blink is complete; the eyelids are closed.

9. The eyelids open slightly, and the eyes are almost looking at the anchor point.

10. Lastly, the eyes lock onto the anchor point, and the eyelids are open like normal.

This look heavy with expressive meaning doesn't work as well without the blinks or with a look that goes in a complete circle:

—— We can add a lot of personality and intent in the look even when the eyes are closing. A subtle animation of the pupil during a blink or as the eyes are closing can be very meaningful.

As with the eye roll from before, pupils moving upward as the eyelids close and downward as the eyelids open gives us subtle information about a look of disagreement, or contempt, yet without making a big action of it. Here, we've added a lot of life, personality, and realism to these eyes.

—— Let's take another example: an attentive, compassionate look. Character A's eyes are focused on a third party (person C who is listening to A and B, for example) as character B is speaking; his eyelids close halfway as his eyes and head move toward B, then his eyes close completely for a few frames, with the head turned toward B. We never see the pupils entirely directed toward B, before the half-open eyes come back to the starting point (person C, who is still listening). We don't see character A look at character B (and he never really looked in a strict sense, since his eyes were closed), but the hint at the eyes new direction under the closed eyelids is enough to convey this effect.

—— A look, to our reptilian brain, can be synonymous with aggression. Non-verbal communication often uses closed eyelids as a sign of peace or approval. Closed eyelids are also a sign of total confidence in a situation: no need for visual inspection or additional information. Here, it's about depicting character's A support, validation, and confidence in what character B is communicating.

— Here is a way to depict a thinking process: first, the eyes look in different directions as if looking for an answer. Then, the look focuses on something ahead; the eyelids close as the idea takes form; After a blink, the face opens up (the eyes arch and the eyebrows raise up very high) to signal the newly formed idea.

— Last example: the look of a character who is about to speak into someone's ear. At the start, the look is directed at the character's companion. Next, the eyes blink and the mouth moves next to the ear. After that, the eyes look in different directions: downward, to the side, upward. The head lifts up occasionally to accompany the mouth, which speaks into the ear while hidden by the hand. This is followed by another blink, and then the character's eyes turn toward the friend again to study their reaction and check that they understood what was said. Then, they continue on with their secret conversation.

One of the reasons the animator acts out the scene on their own is also the need to feel in their own body a very subtle-moving element that may be hard to perceive just by observing someone else. For example, an ear motion, or rather the muscles around the ears. When you have your moment of enlightenment after an intense period of thought, and as your eyes arch upward, try to feel what happens in that spot, right there. Your ears relax: it feels like they fall or move backward on your head. The muscles all around move, and sometimes you feel some movement all the way in your neck. This very subtle motion can help you convey this specific moment to the viewer.

Obviously, the nostrils are not part of a person's look, but they can add meaning to it in a subtle, essential way. Not only can they add an enormous amount of life to your animation when the character breathes, sneezes, etc., but they can also help convey a pent-up anger, a subdued enthusiasm, or a thinly veiled sarcasm.

Without nostril animation

With nostril animation

EXERCISE

▶ **Your character is trying to convince someone about an idea. The person listening to them is off camera (they don't appear in frame); therefore, you'll only be animating your character. The person listening could even be the viewer, which means your character will be speaking directly to the camera.**

The idea your character is advocating does not necessarily have to be conveyed in an intelligible manner either. In fact, the point of this exercise isn't what the character is saying, it's how it's being said: the acting, the expressions, the gestures.

Here, the timing and the facial expressions are key. We need to feel the inner thought, the hesitations, the moments where the ideas become clear or complicated.

Eyelids – Blinking

One might be inclined to think the eyelids are totally mechanical and stripped of any personality whatsoever. However, as we briefly saw before with the eyes and the look, we can manipulate the eyelids' timing, speed, asymmetry and height, as well as with the synchronization/desynchronization with other body parts, to express a number of emotions.

✕ **Let's start with the design and placement of "basic" eyelids:**

— eyes wide open (no eyelids);

— mini-eyelids (often on the character by default);

— eyelids closed one quarter of the way;

— eyelids closed halfway;

— eyelids closed three quarters of the way;

— completely shut (covering the entire eye).

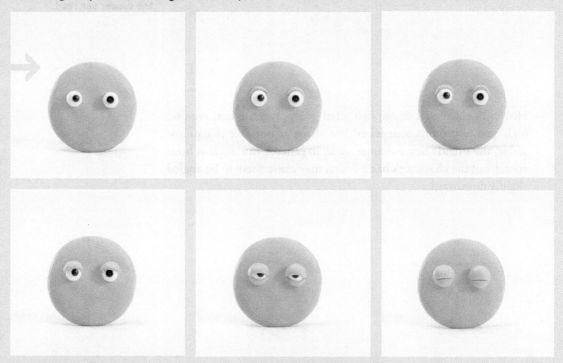

We use the mini-eyelids so we have room to widen the eyes. If there are no eyelids at the start, the eyes are wide open by default, and we can't show any more white. If the chosen design is such that there are no eyelids and we cannot widen the eyes, we have to find other ways to express the same thing with the body (for example, squinting the eyes a few frames in advance, if appropriate, and reopening them wide with an upward or backward head motion to enhance the effect).

We made sure to make the eyelids small by default. When the character is surprised, we can widen the eyes more dramatically by lifting the eyelids.

Here, the character has no eyelids. We are forced to squint the eyes with high and low eyelids and, then, create a contrast with very round eyes without eyelids when the surprise happens, otherwise we have to alter the shape of the face to accompany the surprise and, in this way, create an artificial widening that the viewer can read.

Here is one essential design that often gets put to the test, even on high-quality productions: when the shape of the face is static or stable, the eyelids never change angle. In general, this angle is horizontal, but the character's basic design may cause them to be angled slightly downward.

The eyelids always maintain this angle when they move up and down.

We do not tilt the eyelids inward to show anger,

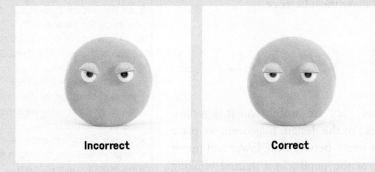

Incorrect   Correct

or outward to show sadness.

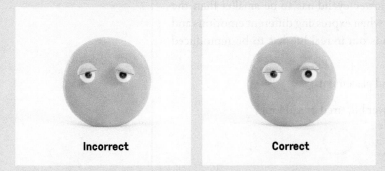

Incorrect   Correct

If you want to give your look more emotion, you need to do it with the other elements at your disposal: the eyebrows, the skin, the skin's wrinkles, the mouth, the eyelid's spacing and timing, the body's language and timing as a whole, etc.

This rule applies to eyes when we cannot modify the shape because they are part of a face whose shape also doesn't change (due to a choice in design or limitation with the materials, as is the case with a rigid puppet).

If the eyes are part of an extremely plastic face (drawn, modeling clay, CGI, etc.) and if the face (the entire head) abides by the laws of stretching and squashing common to the cartoon lexicon (see page 51), then the eyes are going to stretch and squash, too. If this is the case, the eyelids can show an immediate effect in their positioning on the eye. But the effect must be logical and harmonious with the change to the whole face.

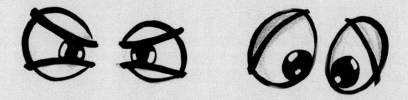

If your eyelids remain in place on closed eyes more than four frames, animate them for more life and realism. The eyes are closed, yes, but did you cushion the closure line between the lower and upper lid? You can provide a little cushioning on the eyelids' closure line by lowering it slightly on the second pose of complete closure. This will help you add a touch of realism that will make the difference.

Don't forget the lower eyelids. They are useful, and it is recommended you create them as part of the design. In general, we place the separating line – if there is one – between the lower and upper eyelids just above the center of the pupils, in a neutral blinking position.

There is no law saying the lower eyelid has to be smaller than the upper eyelid. Anything goes when expressing different emotions and personalities. Whatever stands out in real life has to be reproduced on the character.

Compare these different eyelid placements:

— heavy upper lid, thin lower lid, tired or sad look;

— thin upper lid, thick lower lid, shy or cheerful look.

✖ **Just like with eyes and eyebrows, the eyelids react as a pair: whatever affects one affects the other.**

Nothing happens to one eyelid without it affecting the other, even just a little. Let's take a blink for example: it cannot be animated by lowering one lid over just one eye. Try to wink your eye. Even if you concentrate your hardest and do your best to control your movements, you will not be able to move one eye without affecting the other. Therefore, we animate one eyelid going down completely over one eye in sync with the other eyelid going down slightly over the other eye.

If, on the preceding frames, you made the lower eyelids move upward before a complete closure of the eyes, the direction they are moving in (i.e. the animation curve) will suddenly change in the opposite direction. For this effect to work, we either have to close the character's eyes long enough to ease the change in direction, or reopen the eyes while taking great care to place the lower eyelids lower than the closure line in the preceding frame.

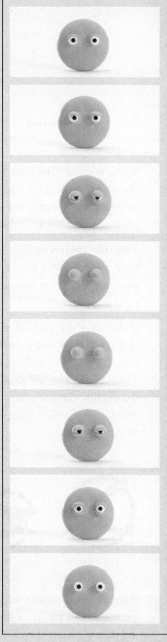

To ensure the eyelids and their relationship is depicted harmoniously, it is recommended you draw (or place) the eyelids' edge on a continuous line between the two eyes, regardless of each eyelid's height. This will automatically keep them connected, and the overall look will be more harmonious and pleasant.

TAKE NOTE!

For a better quality animation, the motion will follow through on the parts of the face close to the eye. The quality often lies in the details and in the number of animation curves in an action's follow-through. For example, in a very big, very emphatic blink with very tightly closed eyelids, the whole face will scrunch together toward the closed eyelids (the mouth will close, the eyebrows will shift toward to the eyes, etc.)

× The language of blinking

In general, we blink our eyes automatically:

— when we turn our head, when we change the direction we're looking in, or what we're looking at;

— when the surface of our eyes needs cleaning (i.e. regularly during neutral moments);

— to protect our eyes from impact;

— when we're tired or drowsy.

Blinking is usually a sign of a conscious brain. We do not blink our eyes when we dream. On the other hand, we do blink our eyes when we come out of a daydream. Similarly, we do not blink our eyes when we are unconscious, or only very slowly (this action can also be interpreted as a desire to leave one's state of unconsciousness and "come back to earth").

Some blinks can be timed so as to be out of sync with the motion of the eyes or the head; when we do this, it gives the blink more significance.

— A character that is anxious or looking for some visual information will look in various directions without blinking; it will only blink after it has left this state. Here, we need to catch as many details as possible, even the most elusive, and even one blink means we could miss some.

— A character surprised by seeing a very fast action out of the corner of their eye will not blink because they will need to immediately analyze what they've seen. The urgency felt in the brain takes precedence over the body's mechanics. The character will blink just after the action.

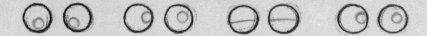

— When the character attempts to understand a situation or person, the blink is also delayed. Indeed, the urgency to analyze takes priority over the body's movements, here, too. The character looks in the desired direction, then moves its head in the same direction; the blink only starts once the head has finished moving.

— On the other hand, a character A doubting what character B is saying will blink its eyes before it starts moving its pupils and head; the eyes will be locked on character B's face, who is talking. We will put a blink of doubt, and then the head will turn toward the point of distraction (character C speaking or some outside occurrence), while the eyes will continue to look at character B. The eyes will then catch up and settle on the new anchor point, and another blink will happen slightly after to signal the end of the thought, i.e. the doubt. Here, character A blinks before turning its head, letting its eyes linger as long as possible on character B in case character B says something or gives off some visual cue that might change character A's opinion.

— Here's one last example that presents a logic worth mentioning, even though, here, the timing is not desynchronized and we are not talking about blinking: The eyelids of a character having trouble hearing or in a noisy environment will always be squinting. When people listen attentively, they tend to squint, as if seeing better will somehow help them hear better (which is entirely possible, given the fact that we always help ourselves by reading lips during our conversations).

Based on these blinking sequences, let's observe different blinking animations for different personalities (for the examples consisting of various expressions or distinct personalities, the language of the rest of the body will be essential).

— **Surprise, worry, enthusiasm, inner conflict:** very fast blinks.

— **Anxiety, fear, disagreement, on the hunt, suspicious**: sparse blinking, even though the eyes change direction a lot.

— **Lazy, tired, nonchalant or bored**: slow to open.

— **Focused on inner thoughts:** the eyes can remain closed for a long time and, then, open slowly (for example, if the character needs to calm down, move onto something else and leave the anger behind).

— **Crazy:** quick, asymmetrical blinks as the eyes open and close.

— **Old, arrogant or contemptuous:** the eyelids are slow and open asymmetrically, or remain asymmetrical over the open eyes. For an old character, it's the motor skills that depict the old age, whereas for an arrogant character, it's about depicting the eye closure (half-closed eyes dissuade people from interacting), the self-sufficiency (the character has no need for anyone), or even the indolent nonchalance (the character has no need to be on alert, since who would mess with them?)

— **In love:** very slow blinks that show trust and soften the aggres siveness of a direct look (we find this trait in animals, and pets in particular).

— **Extremely surprised (in a cartoon context):** double blink on twos (open, closed, open over four frames, closed, half-open, completely open).

TIP!

To accentuate the contrast during an eyelid closure, do not at all hesitate to add small wrin- kles in the corners of the eyes (when the eyes are shut tight).

— **Stuttering** : blinks occur frequently in sync with the stuttering, and the eyes are closed somewhat tightly depending on the will and effort made to relax and get the word(s) out. The look and eyelids return to normal when the word(s) finally come(s) out.

If there is an asymmetrical blink, it has to be animated with one picture per frame so that one eye doesn't catch up to the other too slowly and so that the viewer only perceives it subconsciously.

On an asymmetrical opening, choosing which eye opens first can also provide information or show an intention: opening the eye close to the action first shows impatience, while opening the eye away from the action first shows fear.

ATTENTION!

Learn to distinguish between automatic reflex blinks (on a big change in the eyes' direction, or because the eyes have remained open too long and are, thus, dry) and meaningful blinks (for example, the slow blink of someone in love, or a number of quick blinks indicating the character doesn't understand something). Automatic reflex blinks are important; they must not be underestimated, and we must incorporate them in neutral situations at the right moment. Nevertheless, meaningful blinks take priority. If, for example, you have a need of a meaningful blink six frames away, do not place a reflex blink because it could make the meaningful blink hard to read. Create contrast to make meaningful moments stand out and make them as impactful as possible.

EXERCISE

▶ **Animate an old man seated on a bench, in a park.**

He's looking at the world around him. He is amused, filled with emotion, amazed, or perhaps even angry. We need to sense a story, a situation, on our character's face.

Eyebrows

The eyebrows don't seem too special, and sometimes they don't look like anything more than a simple facial decoration. However, they are actually crucial for human communication. There are many people with very unnoticeable eyebrows who spend a lot of time and energy making them stand out more. This phenomenon isn't just a matter of style, and it has nothing to do with the link often made between the lack of eyebrows and illness. The eyebrows give us essential, precise information about our peers' personality and mindset, and they are an important part of non-verbal communication, too. Therefore, they are an important marker that the animator needs to understand and master.

✕ The first piece of advice is actually more of a warning: keep it simple and be patient. Do not over-animate the eyebrows. Here, too, as with the other elements of an animation, we have to maintain clarity so we can create contrast and impact during important actions and expressions.

For example, we can make downward motions when the eyes are blinking, but they quickly come off as an obvious gimmick. In real life, our eyebrows do not always move as we blink our eyes. Not over-animating guarantees our motions will have more impact when they have a true reason to be there: here, eyebrows animated downward during a blink depict shock, strong emotion. The viewer is, thus, assisted in understanding the scene, in contrast to a blink in an emotionally neutral or low-impact situation.

✕ As we saw before for the eyes and eyelids, the eyebrows influence each other and are dependent on the surface of the forehead. Just like other facial elements (e.g. mustaches, birthmarks, tattoos), we have to imagine them "stitched" to the skin's surface. They only move when the muscles and skin move. The eyebrows are very connected to each other. If one lifts upward, at a minimum the other will lift its closest extremity as a consequence, even if the rest of the eyebrow remains low. It is then in a tilted position.

We can also use the imaginary line here, just like the one we drew for the eyelids. This line moves along the edge of the first eyebrow and follows the curve to connect to the other one.

Line of expression **Placement of the eyebrows** **Refining of the curves**

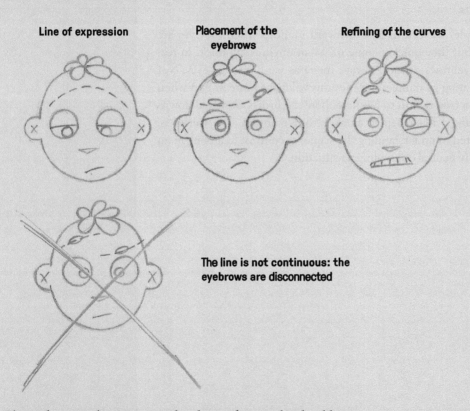

The line is not continuous: the eyebrows are disconnected

The eyebrows only move toward and away from each other like two embroideries on a piece of fabric would. Indeed, a fabric's elasticity is rather limited, just like skin. That is why the eyebrows can only get so far away from each other. Similarly, the eyebrows only get closer if the skin's surface creases and forms folds or wrinkles.

× The eyebrows have a very fast and dynamic animation curve going into a facial expression, and a smooth, rather slow animation curve on the way out (except, of course, if what makes the eyebrows change position is another facial expression, in which case, they come out just as dynamically).

Avoid animating eyebrows downward when the whole face is looking upward (the same applies for any other similar contrast in direction).

Since the animation curve for eyebrows is rather fast, there's a chance you may create the illusion of a "hitch" (a mistake in the animation curve), since your eyebrows are going to move in the opposite direction from everything else over only two or four frames. Try to slow their trajectory or stop their motion to compensate, or even desynchronize the two actions (which is preferable anyhow, if only to help the viewer read it better).

× **A few sets of eyebrows**

Besides surprise, anger and sadness, for which we instinctively draw the line,

there are some other less obvious expressions...

— **Contempt:** the eyebrows are combined with the lowered eye lids to express surprise (the eyebrows) and close-mindedness (low eyelids).

— **Suspicion:** the eyebrows are on a harmoniously asymmetrical line and combined with asymmetrically squinted eyelids.

This expression is a mix of surprise (the raised eyebrow) and disagreement (the lowered eyebrow). The squinted eyelids are a sign of focused, concentrated thought.

— **Pride:** quite often we find this expression associated to a smile in animation films. It conveys a sense of physical or intellectual superiority. Here, the subtly raised eyelids convey a true pride (lowered eyelids tell us the character is sealed off from the world and self-sufficient) or a modest pride indicative of a lack of self-confidence (the wide open eyes yearn for recognition).

— **Compassion:** sad eyebrows (showing empathy in a situation of failure) combine with a weak smile (indicating friendship and support) and open eyelids reflecting attentiveness and kindness toward the other person.

The few examples presented above show the wide range of expressions human look can make. In daily life, these expressions are interpreted accurately by most of us, although rarely consciously. An animator must make a concerted effort to consciously analyze them in order to correctly and accurately depict them in their work.

EXERCISE

▶ **Animate a student working hard on her homework: first she struggles, then she finds a solution, and in the end she tries to keep the results to herself.**

Speech/Lip Sync

Alongside accurate acting with your character, syncing the lips to the speech is contrary to what we've been led to believe by dubbed films, a quick and easy way to breathe life into a character. Naturally, we hear sounds with our ears, but we also "hear" them with our eyes: our eyes read the sounds on the lips. In real life, the sounds and the shape of the lips match perfectly. The technique and the science behind perfect synchronization goes much deeper than it would seem, and it can be absolutely fascinating.

× Creating mouths

In stop motion animation, we often animate the mouths by replacement (see page 31) to save time; this helps avoid modeling each mouth syllable after syllable and, thus, continually remodeling the same mouths over and over.

Each animator will have their own selection of replacement mouths, and each one will correspond to a specific phoneme or sound in their spoken language. One mouth can often be used for several sounds. The following are my mouths (for English):

Ah
Ee
Oo
Oh/Uh
Eh/Ih
R
D/T/S/Z
K/G
V/F
B/P/M
Narrow B/P/M (approaching or returning from Oh, for example)
CH/J
L/N/Th
open neutral
closed neutral

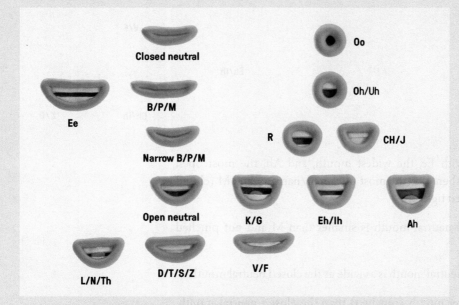

To form the L sound, the tip of the tongue touches the teeth (for realistic animation, the tip goes behind them, but for exaggerated/cartoon animation, it will be more visible on the edge of the top teeth).

The K sound, however, is made by the fleshy/middle part of the tongue, which pushes up against the palate before releasing (it's the release that makes the sound). For this reason, we don't animate the tongue in the same way: the viewer mustn't see the same part stick to the same spot. For the L sound, the tip of the tongue can move upward and touch the teeth without the fleshy part of the tongue moving too much, whereas it's just the opposite for the K sound.

To model mouths more easily and accurately, we first establish
size ratios by making them in the following order:

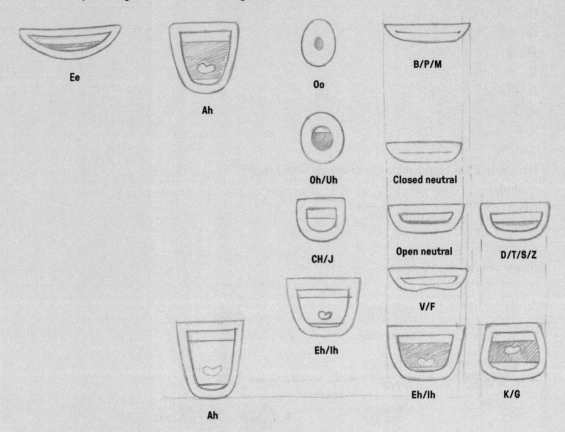

— We start with Ee, the widest mouth, and Ah, the most open
vertically, then Oo (the most puckered/narrow) and M (closed
and pinched tight).

— The closed neutral mouth is smaller than M and not pinched
tight.

— The open neutral mouth is as wide as the closed neutral mouth.

— V is a wider mouth (pinched) than the closed neutral mouth,
but not as wide as M.

— Eh/Ih, K and D/T/S/Z are going to be slightly wider than the
open neutral mouth. We see two rows of teeth, whereas on the
open neutral mouth, only the top teeth are visible.

— Eh/Ih and K are very similar in size, but opposite in shape.

— Additionally, for the K sound, the base of the tongue sticks
to the palate, and we can even show the lower gums with a
stretched lower lip.

— The mouth for D/T/S/Z sounds is as wide as the mouth for
Eh/Ih and K, but it's much more closed, with front teeth that
touch each other without the jaws closing (the molars, which we
do not see, do not touch); the top teeth are just slightly in front
of the bottom teeth.

— From Oo to Eh/Ih, the mouths get bigger as follows: Oo,
Oh/ Uh (no bottom teeth), CH (teeth touch, lower lip forward),
Eh/Ih

— For the L, N and Th sounds, we simply add a tongue in the mouth before/after and animate it as an inbetween.

— The R sound could possibly show more bottom teeth depending on the strength of the sound. If the sound is extremely emphatic, we can use the K mouth.

It is imperative to have the same volume for all the replacement mouths no matter what shape they have. A very open mouth shows stretched lips, whereas a very closed or tightly shut mouth means we'll have plump, thick lips. When modeling, we are therefore going to make sure each mouth has the same weight (see page 102). We can weigh the modeling clay, or we can roll it into one evenly formed sausage that we can divide up into equally thick pieces.

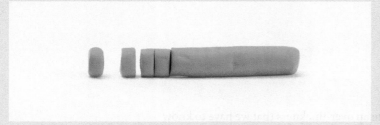

We can also make balls that are equal in size.

Lastly, we can flatten the modeling clay with a pasta machine and cut out identical shapes with a cookie cutter.

Establish where the tension creating the sound is coming from: a low opening, a wide opening, the top teeth, the bottom teeth, both rows of teeth exposed, the lips pulling in one direction, the tongue flat in the mouth, etc.

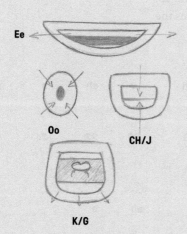

The arrows in the image to the left show the tension on the lips as they push or pull in a given direction, making them thinner or thicker.

We can (we must!) adapt our selection of mouths any time it appears we may need to: change the shape of the mouths (for just one frame, but also if we realize that a mouth is always posing a problem and, therefore, needs changing – what we see on screen is what matters, not what's on a sheet of paper), make a whole new mouth, add/remove mouth elements, for example, the teeth. Nothing is set in stone, so we have to make whatever changes we need to get it right.

In stop-motion animation, 2D mouths (like the "sausage" mouths) must logically still show a minimum amount of depth. Think in terms of bas-relief: the teeth must appear as if they are behind the lips, the tongue behind the teeth, and the back of the mouth behind everything else.

This shallow depth can create an over-thickness that we have to know how to manage so that the lips actually look like they are stuck on the face. We must not hesitate to remove material from the back of them to achieve a convincing design on the overall shape.

On a real body, the teeth are not stuck to the lips. They stick out of the skull and never move from it. The top teeth are totally stationary once they are aligned with the eyes and the nose. Maintain this alignment for all the mouths.

The lips and the lower jaw are animated separately from the skull, and independently from one another. The teeth can disappear behind one or both lips. The lips are not permanently linked together. We do not always show the same amount of tooth surface on every mouth.

✕ Synchronizing picture and sound

The rule of thumb when synchronizing picture and sound over lines of text is to always animate ahead of the sound. Usually, this comes out to be a two frame lead: when we hear the M sound in frame 10, we show the M mouth in frame 8; an Ah sound in frame 12 means the Ah mouth is visible in frame 10.

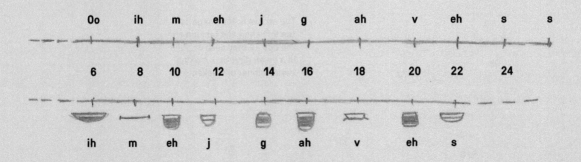

Sometimes, we even go as far as three or four if we need to add a couple frames to hold a sound longer at the exact moment in question or a few frames later.

Let's take the M/B/P and Oo sounds, for example, which are special. These sounds need to stay on the screen longer (ideally, four frames or two poses). The reason for this particularity is the absence of teeth, i.e. the disappearance of a white element that was heretofore rather consistent. If this element (the teeth) only disappears over two frames, the viewer will perceive a hitch i.e. a mistake, and the viewer's eyes won't have time to read the image correctly. The result is a jarring effect.

We also allow more than two frames for these sounds because they are contrasted/extreme sounds that will be present from the moment we hear them, regardless of the accent or way in which they are spoken. Therefore, it is imperative they be shown (especially for M, B and P, no exceptions).

One trick for helping the viewer read the M, B and P sounds: they are easier to read when we make the character's eyes blink at the same time. "Shutting everything" on the face helps the eyes understand these difficult phonemes.

For a line of text spoken in a neutral fashion, a phoneme lasts two frames on average, but this obviously varies depending on the people

BE SURE TO DISTINGUISH BETWEEN THE WRITTEN SOUND AND THE SOUND HEARD

When we're dealing with speech and lip syncing, we never bring to mind the "written" sounds. In fact, when we refer to sounds, we're always referring to the sounds heard. Everyone speaks differently, with their own accent, their own rhythm and their own personality. Our goal is to render these particularities as faithfully as possible to bring the character to life. For example, if we need to say the word "animation" with the obvious M sound in the middle, but the character has just returned from the dentist and is unable to pronounce the M, we will hear "aniVation" or "aniWation." We won't show the M sound. The rule dictating that all the sounds be shown applies to the sounds heard, not the written sounds. In animation, what we hear is all that counts.

and the situation. Listen and calculate ahead of time how to distribute the sounds over the frames.

Lingering on some sounds because they are pronounced longer or because they are strong sounds doesn't prevent us from continuing to animate at 12fps or 24fps. If you lose persistence of vision, which requires us to animate at 24fps, or at a minimum of 12 poses per second, your action will no longer be fluid to the eye. We mustn't use several poses for one sound, otherwise the animation will be jerky.

To avoid falling into this trap, we slightly modify the mouths held over three frames or more so that they are animated at a normal 12fps or 24fps pace.

The body never stops all of sudden, even if it's just a teeny tiny element. If you want to have a big pose over more than two frames, you have to animate the mouth either by emphasizing the phoneme being held out, the subsequent mouth shape, or a combination of the two.

The Ah sound is held over six frames.

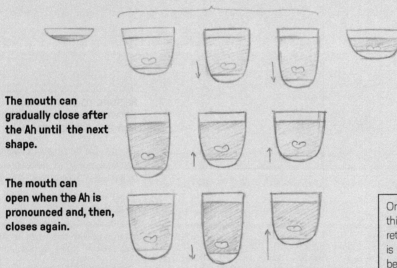

The mouth can gradually open to form the Ah sound.

The mouth can gradually close after the Ah until the next shape.

The mouth can open when the Ah is pronounced and, then, closes again.

Thus, as we've already seen, a mouth shape held over more than two frames continues to be animated over the subsequent poses. We modify it depending on the sound (or absence of sound) that follows, or to emphasize the current sound even more (more tension, more pinched, more open, etc.).

On the other hand, too many evenly spaced inbetweens from one shape to the next or too soft a fluidity lessens the impact of strong sounds. Continuing to animate mouths does not mean having even spacing. The animation could be extremely boring. We want some inbetweens in order to avoid still poses, but we also want strong sounds that contrast with the poses before and after; the inbetweens must therefore be near the extremes.

On an animation curve such as this one here, when we have a return from an extreme pose, it is important that the pose right before and after be different. If they are similar, the extreme pose will look like a "hitch."

Here, mouths 1 and 3 are exactly the same, whereas mouth 3 in the illustration on the left is more closed than mouth 1, which prevents a subliminal image on mouth 2 and makes the whole mouth readable.

Like this:

As opposed to this:

Here's an extreme example that forces the animator to hold the sound for four frames for each successive phoneme. The risk, as we have seen, is that we will lose persistence of vision and have a jerky animation. Here, each of the mouths is modified because all the poses are repeated. The animator modifies the shape a little (in the direction of the preceding or following pose) or creates an interval halfway between the two phonemes, depending on the dynamic intended.

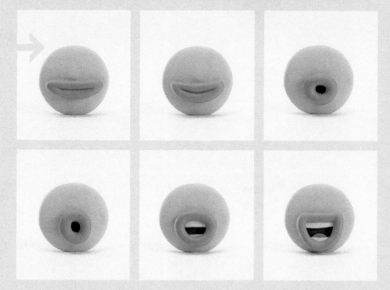

Furthermore, we try not to stay on a sound for less than two frames. One frame per sound is much too short to be perceived by the eye, especially if it is a strong or extreme sound. Leaving a mouth on just one frame isn't really possible except in certain situations.

—— A natural interval between two mouths. Here, the animation curve is not interrupted by the mouth in the middle; thus, we can leave it in without it looking like a mistake.

— Modifying an unreadable mouth ever so slightly, and, thus, making it easier for the eye to perceive (at the same time, we avoid the "subliminal image" effect).

— Placing a mouth "overlapping" two others. Sometimes, a sound must be included, but we don't have enough frames for a mouth to represent it. Thus, we modify the mouths before and after and make them tend toward this half omitted, half shown sound. In the example below, we include the L sound tongue on the second frame of the Oh sound and on the first frame of the Eh sound to represent three phonemes over two mouth shapes.

If we must hold a sound that is prone to producing a "hitch" (like M/B/P or O/U) over just two frames, we will take the first picture of the sound, then slightly animate the shape. Then, we will take the sec ond picture of this sound. The eye will perceive this minimal change, and the sound will be more readable, even though it was held for such a short time.

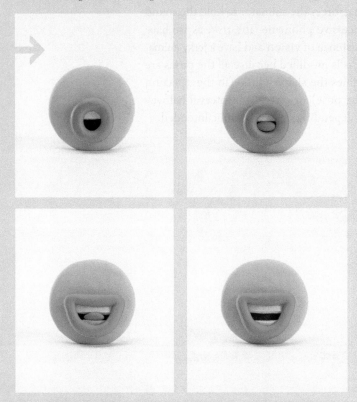

In sum, we always choose to animate with one picture per frame (one pose per frame, instead of one pose per two frames) to make the transitions between the mouths smoother, never to jam lots of different mouths into too few frames.

In general, we animate lip sync with one picture per frame when we want to make a normally hard to read sound readable (M, Oo, F, etc.) and we can only keep two pictures on screen. In this scenario, we take the normal picture and, on the second picture, we "push" the sound a little (the mouth closes more, we tighten the round part of the Oo, the lip of the F bites a little more, etc.).

The tongue is very important and can make the difference between a good animation and an excellent one (real, lively, tangible). It does not disappear as if by magic. It can be inactive for some sounds, but it is still there in the back of the mouth. If it so happens that it is not visible on some mouth shapes, we must absolutely see it (even if inactive) when the mouth is open enough.

In addition to being visible, it must also be animated, it must "move toward" the sound that activates it and move away again if the mouths before and after are open. Do not make the tongue visible on the lone or lone two frames of the "active mouth" (the mouth that requires a tongue to make the sound) and then remove it right away: these frames are likely to create the subliminal effect we mentioned earlier and jar the viewer.

Wrong:

Right:

Also consider showing this tongue in motion toward the active mouth, even if we don't see it when the mouth depicting this sound is posed (D/S/T/Z, for example).

The tongue can be hidden behind the teeth or the lips, but it is nevertheless there to make the sound; we must therefore see it moving toward this sound and moving away from it.

One of the challenges that can make lip sync work fascinating is choosing from among the sounds we hear and the number of frames we have at our disposal: which sounds to show and which ones to omit (and how). The sounds we choose to show are the ones that we cannot avoid making when we, ourselves, form the lip syncing with our own mouth. Weaker sounds hide in the flow of the motion and they are the ones we can omit to pronounce when we form the sound ourselves. In general, consonants are easier to hide within other sounds, and omitting them is less risky. Vowels, on the other hand, must almost always be shown.

Consonants formed inside the mouth (by the throat, or by the tongue, such as K) can be taken out, but sounds formed by the lips (V/F, M/B/P, Oo) cannot.

✕ Acting and animation

The most fundamental thing about lip syncing in terms of acting is first being true to the sound heard, not to the written sound. What is the character saying, what sounds do we actually hear? People have different ways of talking, accents that can be temporary or situational, or even permanent and distinctive. Try not to pay attention to the meaning of what is being said, rather listen as if you did not know the language being spoken so you can be as accurate as possible with the sounds, the intonation and the accent. Then, listen again for meaning to establish the rest of the acting.

Remodel, shape or draw the right mouth based on the intonation, accent, personality, following syllable, or preceding syllable.

When preparing your animation on your exposure sheet, circle the contrasting sounds or words in the character's speech so you can synchronize the timing between the acting and these important moments. Next, on this same sheet draw or describe the head movements, the looks, and any other important gestures to help you keep your acting and your timing under control during the shoot. Finish by organizing the choices you made about the mouth.

Be careful not to "waste" an extreme mouth by using it on a weak or subtle sound when you may need this contrast on a strong sound. For example, in the line of text "on va à la piscine" ("we're going to the swimming pool"), the Ah sound is heard twice in a row, whereas the Ee sound also occurs twice very close together. The Ah of "va" is a strong accent that is going to lead us to animate the body, but the Ah of "à la" is the sound that opens the most. In contrast, the second Ee of "piscine" is both a strong accent and a more open sound than the first "Ee": the lower lip reveals the bottom teeth a little more.

Consonants are less difficult to take out, except the M/P/B sound. As we saw before, this sound is too extreme to be omitted. Even if we hear it very faintly, it must be visible: we only omit it if the sound is completely absent. Indeed, we must make sure we don't give the viewer the impression something is off.

WATCH OUT

Certain sounds (like T or B) are perceptible when the mouth releases the tension. We must, therefore, show these mouths before we hear the mouth pop or click open.

EXERCISE

▶ **Here is a line of text: "The children left too early this morning."**

Record yourself. Listen to this line of text and analyze it. Make your choices, calculate as best you can, and then put the mouths in the right places on your exposure sheet.

*Share your creations on social media with **#SecretsoftheAnimator***

ON – V – A – A – L

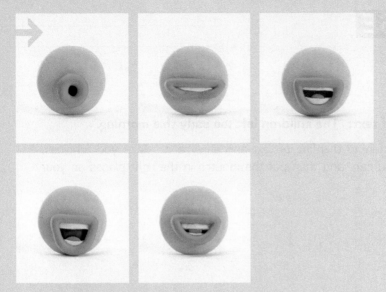

Ah (two frames for the moving tongue) – P (two frames to "push" the sound) – Ee

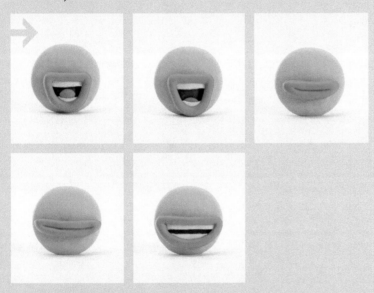

S – Ee – N (the sound is released as the tongue moves)

In the same vein, if two exactly similar sounds are only separated by one other sound (e.g. "papa," "maman," "minimum" ("daddy, "mommy," "minimum"), we try to not use the same shapes to depict these two sounds in order to avoid the "subliminal image" effect in the middle. Thus, we alter the shape of one sound compared to the other (for example, we modify the first Ah compared to the second Ah of "papa," depending on the intonation and which of the two sounds is strongest) so that the shape in between (here, P) does not result in a "hitch" and come off as a subliminal image. As we saw before, we never pronounce the same sounds in the exact same way. The intonation evolves over the course of the word; the intensity of a sound is accented or restrained, and it is always possible to identify the stronger of two identical sounds.

P – Ah – P – Ah

M – Ah – M – An

M – Ih – N – Ih – M – Uh – M

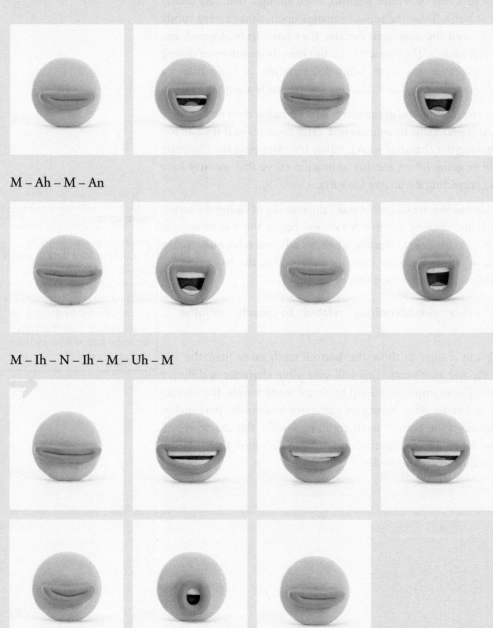

Most of the time, the lips are animated ahead of the sound, especially when the character is in the process of thinking or hesitating. The shape of the mouth changes and reflects what is going on inside the character's head before it decides to express the words or sound. We can observe this phenomenon practically every day in the common hesitation that precedes "well uh." We can see, sometimes for a long moment, the perfectly silent "Oo" (w) of a mouth tightly puckered as the character hesitates before speaking.

For each sound, look closely at the sounds that follow. Indeed, the shape of your mouth will more often be influenced by the sounds that follow than by the ones that come before, except if there is a hesitation or special circumstances.

Similarly, it is very rare for someone to abruptly stop speaking by immediately shutting their mouth. In your animations, avoid automatically shutting your characters' mouths right after the last syllable they speak. In general, the mouth usually stays open well after the last syllable (in terms of frames, i.e. fractions of a second, not automatically in terms of whole seconds, even though that can clearly happen as well). Thus, the mouth remains open, though very subtly animated, until the character decides they have truly stopped and closes their mouth. The character can also have its mouth open during an entire exchange, like a very animated argument or when there's a big confusion. The magic word for our animations is always the intent.

It is better to ease the end of the text too much rather than not enough. Indeed, it is preferable to animate one extra pose (even if it's one too many, making the character weak), rather than stopping the character too early or going off on another animation curve that we may have difficulty correcting if it arrives too early.

For a body motion, we can often make the mistake of easing the action too much and sucking out the dynamism, but at the end of speech, we rarely run this risk. Generally, when we talk, we relax our mouths slowly. In addition, the more extreme the sound is, the more time we need to allow inertia to return (see pages 40-42).

TAKE NOTE!

When a character shuts its mouth right after the last sound comes out, it's a true sign of intent. Depending on the context and the body language, the character could be thinking, for example, that there is nothing left to be said, neither by them nor anyone else.

A few other considerations related to speech, mouths and acting

— We can choose to show the bottom teeth more than the top teeth, and vice-versa. This will give your character a different look. For example, if the top teeth are more visible, the character will come off as having an aggressive or sarcastic personality, whereas if the bottom teeth are more visible, the character will give off an air of suspicion and arrogance, a look that they are cer-tain of their knowledge.

— What sounds go along with loud inhaling and exhaling? Do not forget to animate an inhaling or exhaling mouth when it seems necessary, and don't forget the rib cage, either (when possible). All these little details make the difference and make your character even more credible to the viewer. To animate the rib cage, a slight adjustment to the clothing or the modeling clay on the body's surface is enough.

— The smile looks sincere when it comes mainly from the eyes. This means that a smile changing from a closed mouth to an open mouth is animated by moving the upper lip, and not by lowering the lower lip. In the chain reaction, the eyes squint, and the cheeks move and pull the smile upward.

However, don't tense the lips on a smile too much, otherwise it could turn into a forced smile. In particular, ease the tension on the lower lip and open the space between the top and bottom teeth ever so slightly.

— Very often, with replacement mouths, we forget to animate the upper lip because we're busy changing the lower jaw. However, this lip does not stay still! Keep your character's real anatomy in mind! Don't be lazy, and don't be parsimonious with your time. We have to animate the upper lip in accordance with the mouths used. The lips of an Ah mouth moving to an Oo mouth will show narrow lips, top and bottom, whereas when an Ah mouth moves to a D, the upper lip also changes, albeit more subtly.

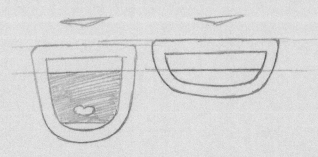

The lip stretches and shifts up over the teeth, which remain aligned.

EXERCISE

Here is a line of text to animate: "I didn't find the key."

Record yourself saying this phrase in different ways based on different emotions (you can add any hesitations, laughter or breathing you deem appropriate).

Animate your character by changing its acting (its attitudes, expressions, postures, funny faces and ways of talking) based on these different emotions.

▶ **In a panic, right before going out.**

▶ **In a confiding tone.**

▶ **Laughing.**

▶ **Embarrassed.**

▶ **Angry.**

Share your creations on social media with #SecretsoftheAnimator

MOVEMENT WITH A PERSONALITY

Let's take basic walking and running,

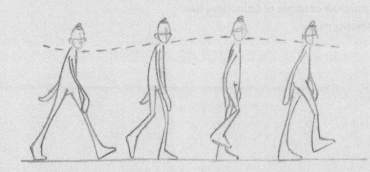

and see what elements will be altered by giving them distinctive features.

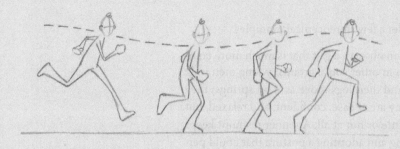

× First and foremost, it's important to point out that it is always possible to make a character move, even if we theoretically don't have the means. Indeed, anything that isn't possible in real life is totally possible in animation. Does the character have no feet? He can walk and move about, all the same. No eyes? He can see and look surprised. It's all about choosing the replacement elements. The famous lamp created by Pixar is a great example, both in how it moves without limbs and in its facial expressions, even though it has no face.

× The element we choose to direct our walking motion will have a lot to say about our character's personality.

When the arms move and carry everything else, the character comes off as bustling, in control, focused. If it's the legs that set the tempo, the character is more relaxed, slow-going, as if it's letting life call all the shots, going from one happy coincidence to the next. When the pelvis is the driving force behind a fast walk with locked joints, the character is doing its best to hurry up; it's late for something, and it's walking as fast as it can. On the other hand, a pelvis that rolls over a slow walk, with flexible joints, is more an example of seduction, like when we create a certain female stereotype.

To illustrate this, lets consider a few stereotypical examples.

— At music festivals, we can observe a gait that is much more common in metal fans than in other social groups: young men walk very tall and straight, and their legs move as if on springs; they give the impression they are at ease, confident, and relaxed, but their ams swing very little or not at all. An inner restraint keeps them from fully relaxing and adopting a posture that could perhaps be perceived as extravagant. There remains a fair amount of control in their motions.

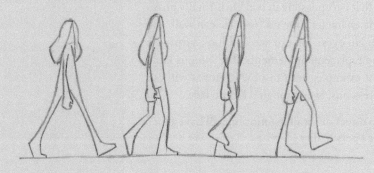

— Now and then, we have the misfortune of observing a duo (a couple or just friends) in the street trying to score a dose of drugs. Here, the individual gaits are interesting, but the dynamic of the two people together is even more interesting. The duo is clearly on a mission. One is focused and looks quite unfriendly; he walks straight ahead, quickly, with rather long strides. It's an efficient, albeit slightly ravaged gait. By contrast, the other person looks wretched, plaintive, troubled. He leans over toward his friend and talks while walking. His pleading body places him in a position of inferiority. He also takes twice as many steps as his companion to keep pace. His gait is nervous and chaotic.

THE "RAVAGED" GAIT

What does a "ravaged" gait consist of? Here, it's the lack of muscle control in the body and limbs while the character is moving. Much like the gait of a drunk person, the limbs do not move fluidly, and the joints do not position themselves in a naturally controlled fash ion. For example, we perceive a very slight change in the left/ right knee, which, as an aftermath, leads to a slight hesitation on the pelvis as the foot impacts the ground and the center of gravity shifts. Sensory informtation is also affected, and distances and speed aren't always measured right. Feet might not lift up enough and will scrape the ground just a little more on some steps. It is also possible to have a step with a varying number of poses (breaking, in this way, the steady pace of a traditional gait) if the leg has been thrust too far forward or too close, and the person "falls" over their own feet. All of these little details are very interesting to observe and note down.

✕ The more their arm and hand joints move, the more the character seems female. The arms (from the shoulder to the elbow) barely swing, the forearms move somewhat more, and the hands are extremely flexible. To make the gait more masculine, we lock these joints.

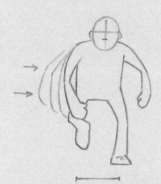 

The arm's joints are locked, the gap between the feet on the ground is wide.

The arm's joints are flexible, the gap between the feet on the ground is reduced (or even on the same line).

By contrast, a female or feminized character will take small steps and have no gap between their legs, or their legs will cross over, whereas a male or masculinized character will take bigger steps and have a much bigger gap between their legs.

The strides of a character showing "masculine" characteristics are bigger compared to a character showing "feminine" characteristics, which will have smaller strides.

✕ In the walk cycle, we can say the arms are "dead" when they swing in response to the motion of the legs. On the other hand, we will say they are "lively" when they are active and give energy to the legs. The intent is totally different, and the swinging of the arms does not synchronize with the legs in the same way: the active ("lively") arms are slightly ahead compared to the passive ("dead") arms. They are also straighter, with stiffer joints and a smaller angle compared to the "dead" arms, which are more flexible and dangle more.

✕ In animation, weight is essential, especially when considering a character's timing and animation curves. The heavier an element is, the more energy it requires to move: the motion is slower and subject to greater inertia, which has accumulated. Consequently, the motions are also not as big, either.

Running with heavy weight is a good example: the body squashes a lot and for a long time on poses where the legs switch and hardly raise up when the legs are extended.

✖ **A few other particular movements worth mentioning**

— The frightened cartoon (exaggerated)-style run: the pose is high and the weight is on the left leg while the right leg is raised at the back, then the pose is low with the weight on the left leg while the right leg is raised forward, and vice-versa (a high pose with the weight on the right leg while the left leg is raised at the back, then a low pose with the weight on the right leg while the left leg is raised forward).

— A slow, suspicious, intimidating military inspection: here, we are going to increase how long the foot stays in the air before it touches the ground and the general moves on to the next soldier. What we get is a leg extended forward in the air for quite a long time before the back leg moves forward, which happens more quickly, creating a contrast.

— A skip: what creates the skip is the small additional jump of the foot on the ground while the foot in the air is moving forward from behind.

— A character climbing a ladder. The limbs move in the following sequence: the left leg, then the left arm with the body's weight shifting downward in anticipation; next, the character lifts itself upward while it transfers its center of gravity to the left side; then, the right leg, the right arm, the downward anticipation, and lastly the body's weight shifts up and to the right.

✕ Do not hesitate to move your character enough during a movement from one point to another so that we won't get the impression it's expending a lot of energy for very little effect. On the other hand, if you move the character forward too much from frame to frame, particularly during a run, it may be hard to read, and what you'll get is a double exposure/strobe effect. If this is the case, it is often recommendable to animate with one pose per frame (24fps).

EXERCISE

▶ **What are these poses telling us?**

_____

_____

_____

_____

See the solutions at the end of the book.

Body Language – Attitudes

Think about placing your character in a context. What happened just before the shot? And just before that? What's going to happen after? What's happening off camera and how does that affect your character? Modify your character's poses, the direction it's looking in, its faces and its attitude based on all of this. The viewer needs to understand the context from the very beginning of the shot. This sets the tone for the scene. Think about your lines of action, how you would do this in a drawing. Don't use weak poses that don't say anything, or poses with multiple lines of action (which are, therefore, hard to read).

What follows is a list of observations from real life or particular traits I have had to animate. These examples are either an object lesson in the kind of attention you need to pay to everyday attitudes and gestures, or particularly rare cases worth pointing out and mentioning here.

✗ Do not forget that the human brain never rests. Thoughts come out one after another like an assembly line, like nursery rhymes that use the end of one word to star another. Good acting is acting that makes us feel this chain of thoughts and emotions.

✗ Unlike a person who must absolutely convince their audience, a person who is very factual in their speech does not move much. They are not moved by passion or emotion. The facts are all too familiar for them to draw emotion or energy from them. We already mentioned (page 133) the fact that such a person is much more likely to look people in the eyes while speaking: their brain, which knows exactly what comes next, has no need for the neutral space that looking into the void provides when thought is required. The person's face and body won't move very much, either. The eyebrows, eyelids, and eyes are steady; the joints are completely locked; the body is stiff and the range of motions is extremely limited. When the body moves, it's just as automatic as the speech itself: the motions are very limited in range and very controlled. They just help emphasize the words that the person considers to be important.

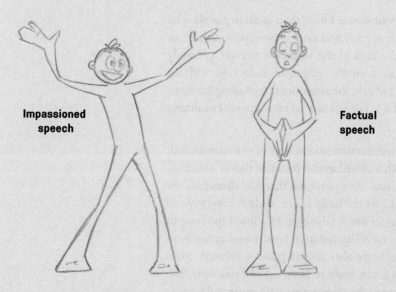

Impassioned speech

Factual speech

✕ We saw on page 126 that it is better to avoid acting out every little thing that is explicitly said, whether it be said by the character or a voice-over. This doesn't allow for a realistic or interesting animation. Exploiting both levels, inner and outer, allows us to feel the character's complexity.

In the same way, no one looks at what they point at. Your character can look first, then point while looking at the person it's interacting with, or not look at all. This shows the viewer that the character knows exactly where the object in question is. The character can look at it again to check that it's still there, but not when it's pointing at it.

✕ The game of seduction is a fascinating situation. The next time you are waiting for your friends at a restaurant or café, don't take out your telephone. Look around you. Identify any individuals, couples or groups who are in a game of seduction. Analyze whatever details make you think this. These details are the key to the attitudes you'll want to reproduce in your own animations.

On page 147, we talked about slower blinks than usual in people who want to convey a message of trust and non-aggressiveness. Indeed, these slow blinks soften the look of the seductive person, precisely because that person focuses on the object of seduction without hardly ever looking away (which, for any animal, including humans, is a very aggressive sign if it is not attenuated by some other calming sign).

The person attempting the seduction makes a lot of eye contact and, thus, very slow blinks, with a closed eyelid position that is a fraction of a second slower than usual. Any potential threat is eliminated by these signs, which suggest that the body is not ready for any type of conflict (too slow) or counterattack (the eyes are closed too long to notice a danger). We are in a relationship of trust based entirely on the facial expression. The body also adopts passive, relaxed poses indicating that the person is not ready to jump up and run away. The body is totally oriented toward the other person. It is near and leaning forward. The head is tucked into the shoulders and, often, tilted to the side (especially when listening, but sometimes throughout the whole interaction, too, when the person wants to show big signs of non-aggressiveness).

TIP!

When we tilt the character's head to express an emotion, be sure to do it where the neck meets the lower jaw. When we tilt the neck at its base where the neck and shoulders meet, we give the viewer the impression that the character is trying to look at something situated behind an element that is in the way.

In the realm of seduction, signs of submission are particularly visible in an upward, more child-like gaze that voluntarily puts itself in a position of inferiority (hierarchy is often translated in terms of height: the smaller, the less potentially threatening).

A dominant, controlled position, on the other hand, is going to result in the eyes being placed higher so as to convey assurance and self-confidence.

Submission　　　　　　　　　　　　　　　　　　**Domination**

The body is also going to be straighter. Striking the right balance between the self-confident body and the relaxed, less aggressive body is often a matter of timing in the interaction. Thus, often the body will look confident when a person is speaking and relaxed when the same person is listening.

There is a wide range of attitudes and behaviors out there, so pay very good attention to the messages that non-stereotypical, "outside-the-box" people are sending you. Do you see a childlike woman, a femme fatale, a strong and independent woman, etc.?

Do you see a domineering man, a playboy, or an easy-going man who accepts equality?

Do you see people who abide by gender roles and social hierarchy? How are these concepts conveyed by their attitudes?

In addition to the pact of non-aggression adopted by the body language, we can also observe the language of desire, which results in a large number of looks at the mouth and other parts of the face (e.g. the hair) but, also, lots of tactile gestures knowingly made to the rhythm of the signs that the other person sends back.

Gazes towards the body are extremely interesting to observe because they will be perceived as aggressive or encouraging depending on the context of the interaction. They will generally be made with extreme caution. In fact, if they aren't made carefully enough, if there are too many, if they are too exaggerated, there are immediate consequences.

✕ We've just looked at the notions of domination and submission and how they relate to seduction, but we mustn't forget that they are very much present in all social interactions, even if deliberately reduced in scenarios of equality. It is interesting to note that in a position of superiority, a character must not lower its eyes toward the ground. We keep the line of sight higher than that of the other characters. If, however, the character in a position of superiority does look downward, it will tend to compensate with an upward head movement and very low eyelids to confirm its rejection of openness and the impossibility of a threat against it.

✕ Hysterical laughter between two or more characters is more pronounced and more lively if we animate the ones who are fueling the hysterical laughter, in particular when they look at each other and laugh even more. Opening the eyes partially and asymmetrically – in an attempt to open the eyes and calm down, which is abruptly interrupted by another burst of laughter – will be even more effective.

The stages are as follows: character A opens one eye to take a peek at character B, then, as its first eye finishes opening, its other eye begins to open. At this point, the eyelids are still quite visible. Character A immediately plunges forward again and starts laughing even harder; its eyes are shut and its eyelids very tight.

✕ A jolt move is going to put all the principles of anticipation, rebounding and energy transfer into action and will require separate animation curves for each of the body's elements, as we saw on page 15. The body erupts in a sudden backward motion and then collects itself in a tenser, tighter position than before. If we consider the distance between the lowest and highest pose over the whole motion, and if we divide the difference into five height levels, the motion happens as follows:

neutral pose at 2; outburst at 5; return at 1; ease with rebound at 2, then 3.

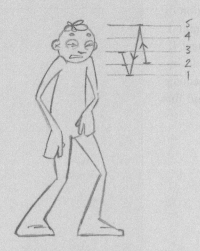

On the other hand, the surprise (or the shock) will show an almost inverse motion. The body will squash itself in anticipation of a backward stretch, and the height will remain unchanged for as long as takes the mind to analyze the new situation:

neutral pose at 2; anticipation at 1, then at 0; stretch at 5; slowdown with rebound at 4, then 3.

Once again, be sure to pay attention to the time of your actions. For example, a shocked or extremely surprised person takes longer to recover (several seconds), even if the object of the shock itself has returned to normal.

✗ It is interesting to note that when people scratch their skin out of nervousness, discomfort, insecurity or shyness, they don't really scratch their skin in the same way as if they were stung by something or had an itch; they rub themselves with the flat part of their fingers. Observe what these motions really look like in real life. The decision to animate a real motion or a motion of our collective unconscious will clearly have to be made knowingly, and not out of any habit that may be totally inappropriate within the context of your own scene. Along the same line, it is common to see that in instances of intense listening or daydreaming, people rub their skin without thinking about it (the arm, the jaw, the neck, etc.)

✕ A finger that scratches the character's head during a deep thought can be broken down into a loopable six-pose move:

— 1. extended;

— 2. over-extended, moving downward;

— 3. lowered;

— 4. at its low point;

— 5. curled downward;

— 6. curled at its high point.

The small finger is the leading finger, the one that gets the looped motion started. Then, each finger moves one pose behind their neighbor (when the small finger is animated in pose 6, the ring finger is animated in pose 5, the middle in pose 4 and the index in pose 3).

✕ It is totally possible to add small touches of realism to accentuate the characteristics and particularities. For example, the character can push its glasses back up from the end of its nose or swallow its saliva after a big effort.
Subtle hand and finger motions can also add a lot of life without, however, over-animating. They work kind of like a punctuation mark. A foot motion can also be used in the same way. That said, be careful to only use these animations in appropriate, meaningful situations so you don't drown out your contrasts and big moments,

as we saw on page 47.

Thus, hands together between the legs in a seated position are going to denote a sense of discomfort but also a desire to not take up space. Hands placed in the underarms, on the other hand, can convey a freezing sensation, or an attitude of domination. Analyzing the rest of the body language will help determine which.

A foot that begins to shake feverishly while the character is listening to a friend reveals a sense of nervousness or agitation, perhaps because of guilt or pent-up anger. The foot can also twist to indicate embarrassment, or suddenly stretch out at the same time as a word or motion we want to emphasize. In this last example, the motion is not a vehicle for any subconscious message; it simply helps draw the viewer's attention at an important moment.

The viewer probably won't look at all these little gestures directly, but the visual information will enter the viewer's peripheral vision and be meaningful, even if subconsciously. All these subtle poses are laden with visual messages, and they are fascinating to study and reproduce.

✕ Inactive body elements are very often mirroring another element that, just the opposite, is very active. For example, an inactive hand will reflexively, and much more subtly, imitate the motion of an active hand that, for example, tries to catch a thrown object out of the air at full speed. The fingers will tighten, and there will be a small translational motion as well, in addition to the motion generated by the transfer of energy and the body's inertia.

ADVICE

Do not forget to desynchronize to make the animation harmonious and natural, especially on elements that move in pairs (the arms, the hand/eyes duo, etc.). Determine which element is leading and which is following, and make the actions overlap so the overall motion is nice and fluid.

EXERCISE

Now it's your turn, using the technique of your choice, pose your character in the different contexts below:

▶ innocent at the police station;

▶ guilty at the police station;

▶ a police officer listening to a suspect's statement;

▶ a police officer in training listening to the same statement.

Share your creations on social media with **#SecretsoftheAnimator**

ANIMATION
OF NON-HUMAN
CHARACTERS

The challenge, when animating non-human characters, is two-fold. Above all, the first challenge is to make them human! Because the viewer understands the human codes of verbal and non-verbal language, naturally our characters must, therefore, appear to abide by the same codes, no matter if they are objects or animals. How we handle this will vary based on our character's nature and initial design. The second challenge can also be complex: it's about knowing how our character functions so that we can combine it with the personality, the expressions, and the acting in a way which fits the project and how it was conceived. These animations are some of the most interesting to work on and are very popular with viewers.

When a character is an object, the almost mandatory rule is to give it human, though sometimes animal, qualities so that the viewer will relate and empathize with it. If your character does not move like a human at least in some way (regardless of its design), you will create a distance between it and the viewer.

No matter the shape and function, we have to attribute human communication qualities to many of the object's elements and establish a motion and movement chart so that we can reproduce typical gestures and body language.

The presence and absence of recognizable body elements

✕ If you animate an object into which human face elements have been incorporated, that's one less thing to worry about because the main source for communicating and expressing emotions has already been provided to you. All that's left for you to do is explore its motions and a timing that work well for this object. And, then, make the acting as accurate as possible in spite of any elements that might be missing. For example, your object might not have any eyebrows or hands.

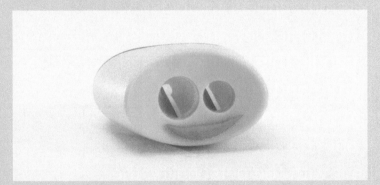

✕ If the object is missing a face or body elements, you can make use of a very helpful biological fact here: the human brain, in general, is particularly well skilled at creating connections everywhere. Thus, the viewer will have a natural tendency to see faces, arms and legs even if we only give the slightest hint of them. In this way, we can use the different colors of some Post-it® notes or a Rubik's Cube®, and we can easily give it a face or other elements conveying communication (see next page).

✕ For objects lacking any internal element capable of being rearranged to form a face, we look for an element in the design itself. For example, a car has headlights, which look like eyes, and a radiator grill, which looks like a mouth. We can also rely on the basic natural placement of the face in relation to the body: an easy chair will have feet that we will consider as such, and consequently the

EXERCISE

▶ **Animate a house with no face.**

Use the light in the windows for the eyes, turn the door into a mouth, etc.

seat will be looked on as the body, and the backrest will naturally be associated with the head. The face will obviously be missing, but an easy chair is a mobile object (indeed, it can raise up, turn around, move, etc. be it with its wheels, by hopping, swaying from left to right, or even sliding). Thus, all the head motions considered meaningful to humans can be applied here.

With no identifiable body or face element, we apply the same rules as we do for non-deformable objects (see pages 193-197).

Transformable/Malleable/Deformable Objects

Objects we can change the shape of are easier to animate than those whose shape is solid and unchangeable. Some things have a naturally malleable shape, such as bread dough, a handful of paper clips (which can react like a school of fish or one big monster), a backpack, or a necklace.

Others have a more solid shape, like a glass bottle or a wardrobe. It is nevertheless possible to alter them artificially by drawing, CGI, or using soft materials like modeling clay or silicone.

It is important to keep in mind the physical particularities of each object, just like we would for a human. We will not animate a necklace in the same way as a dresser. One is light and slippery, like a snake, the other is heavy and hard to move, like a sumo wrestler.

EXERCISES

▶ Animate two sponges arguing about which one is the "dominant male."

▶ Animate twenty paper clips moving from one point to another.

Moreover, it is important to give the object a personality. Such a personality can come from any ideas or concepts associated with the object, like the teapot in *Beauty and the Beast*, which is very motherly and traditional. In this way, a fountain pen might seem older, or richer, than its wooden companion, the pencil.

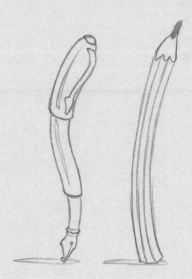

A horse saddle might very well talk and act like a cowboy. White paper might be delicate and fragile, while a piece of sheet metal will be strong and firm. On the other hand, the paper will be adaptable and flexible, whereas the sheet metal will be stuck in its ways or beliefs.

These objects, with or without an identifiable face or limbs, are transformable by design. All action lines, big poses and important curves are allowed here (within the design's limits, of course). And this doesn't include everything we can do with space and timing, which remain the animator's ultimate tools especially when other ones are non-existent.

> **TAKE NOTE!**
>
> The personality of the object can totally vary from what we might expect, but it must still be logical, coherent and consistent throughout the film, with or without variations/evolutions.

Non-deformable Objects

Whether by choice or due to technical constraints (a glass purchased at a shop for a stop-motion animation film, for example) non-deformable objects probably pose the most interesting challenge for an animator: we have to bring to life an object without any human elements or any way of modifying its shape to create curves and lines that would make it easier to read. Nevertheless the animator must still find a way to stir empathy and emotion in the viewer.

To overcome this challenge, we will need to use motions that have a clear and readable intent, and our timing must be spot on. This timing/motion tandem must be good enough to depict typical situations. As mentioned above, space and timing are the ultimate tools for an animator when there's nothing else left. By "space" we mean the movements from one spot to another (translations in space) but also the motions on the object (rotations, tilting).

Thus, when the character doesn't have recognisable human shapes, we will use typical human timings, easily identifiable lines of actions, or iconic acting motions that apply to the whole human body rather than parts of it, and that we will transfer onto our object as a whole, without the use of a face or limbs.

× For example, what's a characteristic of shyness? Naturally, the head and face of a conventional character will make furtive glances upward and blink its eyelids uncontrollably. However, shyness is also, and perhaps mainly, defined by the timing and the space. Below is a sequence from a scene with a tube of lipstick shyly approaching a trophy:

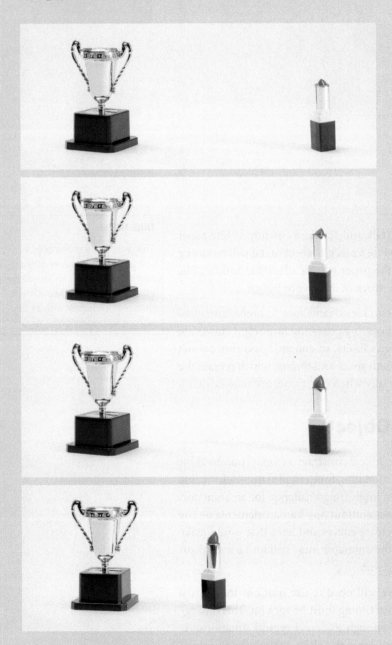

—— **The timing** (depicted by the animation curves and a sequence of different expressions of body language):

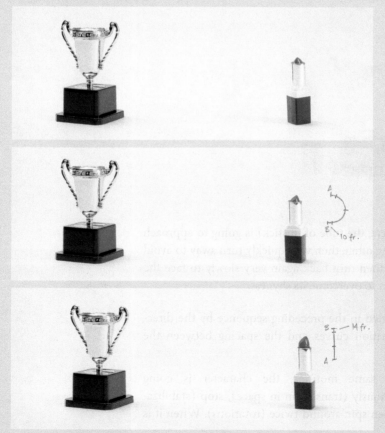

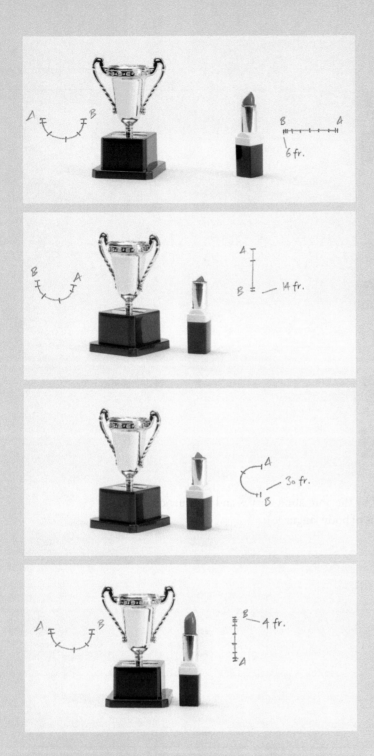

The character (here, the tube of lipstick) is going to approach gradually, stopping often, then very quickly turn away to avoid eye contact, and then turn back again very slowly to face the trophy, in an effort to overcome its shyness.

— **The space** (depicted in the preceding sequence by the direction of the animation curves and the spacing between the characters).

If we use the same motions, the character is going to approach cautiously (translation in space), stop (stabilization in space), then spin around twice (rotations). When it is very close, it will very likely shift "from one foot to the other," hesitating shyly.

Our object has no malleable body or face to depict emotion. And yet, there is emotion. The viewer recognized the timing common to this type of situation and the movements in space that resonate with the viewer's own experience. The viewer can relate. The animator triggered a sense of empathy; they succeeded at putting the viewer in the shoes of a tube of lipstick in love with a trophy.

✕ Let's consider another example: anger. If we forget about furrowed brows, extreme mouth motions or big, exaggerated arm motions, anger is characterized by fast movements, abrupt stops, and a dynamic, intermittent, and sometimes shaky timing. What follows are totally exaggerated motions all over the body and an aggressive, invasive conception of personal space that seeks to establish a certain superiority at all times.

The jar of herbs suddenly approaches a jar of spices, then leans in aggressively by eliminating any personal space. Its top opens: its face appears higher than the spice jar's face. The jar of herbs clearly appears to have an intimidating attitude.

EXERCISES

▶ **Animate a pair of glasses trying to hit on a flask.**

▶ **Animate a pair of compasses moving from one point to another (use a surface like cork or a foam mat to help you not lose contact with the ground).**

Share your creations on social media with #SecretsoftheAnimator

A character of this type requires an approach similar to human character animation (animation described in the previous chapters), with the exception that we must keep two additional aspects in mind (depending on the film's needs and the director's requirements).

✕ We are going to try to maintain the animal qualities, or, otherwise, play on contrasts by reversing the stereotypes associated with the animal in question or the characteristics of its body.

✕ We are also going to have to animate specific body parts on the animal (parts we don't find on humans), but in a way that it looks like a human as much as possible for the viewer.

This isn't just about generating empathy in the viewer (necessary for them to get involved in the character's story), it's also about conveying that our character is not simply a human in an animal outfit: it's more of an animal with humanized movements and communication.

Preserving and Experimenting with Animal Qualities

During the production of *Creature Comforts*, a series filmed at Aardman Animations and based on Nick Park's famous short of the same name, the animator, Sam Marti, was tasked with animating a gorilla character, and his performance was a home run. Indeed, what he animated was a gorilla, not just a human in a gorilla outfit. The character oozed testosterone from every pore, and the muscular power of its body was palpable. It had such an unfriendly personality – albeit sarcastic and witty – that we were happy to be on the other side of the screen.

Sam Marti specifically animated the hands to match the gestures and body language of gorillas: cracked fists, hands hanging heavily, fingers curled up (almost) all the time, and very big, heavy gestures.

This is why, before starting an animation, it is important to identify the physical and biological characteristics of the animal in question, as well as all of its related behaviors. Run a few Internet searches, and you'll get a good view of what you need, along with some unique details to create the character's recurring particularities. Aside from all the scientific and encyclopedic pages, it is essential to study videos and establish a set of references. It is also important for your body to experience timings, different gestures, and any typical movements by reproducing what you see for yourself, to the extent you physically can. First, observe an animal in a given situation and imitate it, then try to transfer this to the situation you plan to animate.

The combination of behaviors and biological particularities already provide a ton of ideas on how to build the character. To these behaviors, we are going to add any related stereotypes or any impressions about the personality based on any particular physical traits. Do we see a powerful, very masculine animal consistent with the stereotypes and look of a gorilla? Do we want to show the fragility of the butterfly, the speed of the cheetah, or the flexibility and slyness of the snake?

This raises the question of whether we should use these characteristics and information. We can choose to create a character that reflects all of these particular traits, but we can also choose to go against these stereotypes to create a contrast, and even some humorous situations.

A delicate butterfly can totally be a man that oozes testosterone. Maybe it hits the gym anytime it has a spare half hour in its busy executive schedule.

Building a character is a fascinating and enriching psychological adventure.
Like with a human character, the important thing is to be coherent and logical. We have to maintain the personality for the entire duration of the film even if the character evolves and we chose to gradually reveal information about its past, its personal context, and its inner conflicts. All these elements contribute to the character and influence its attitudes and motions at all times, even at the start of the film, when the viewer hasn't yet received the keys to understanding them.

EXERCISE

Film yourself imitating these animals.
Your body's exact shape in space is not the priority; concentrate on the animal's characteristics.

- **a caterpillar**
- **a squirrel**
- **a chameleon**
- **a bear**

These animals are real estate agents. The situation is the visit of an apartment.

Share your creations on social media with **#SecretsoftheAnimator**

Integrating Specific Body Parts

How do we harmoniously integrate foreign body parts to humans? And how do we give meaning to visual and bodily communication so that a viewer can understand it. Observation is also essential, here, because animals don't all use one part of the body in the same way, nor do they have the same system of communication. For a foreign body part, or parts, it is important to make a motion chart. Even if the body part isn't necessarily biologically accurate, it adds a degree of non-verbal communication that will become one of the character's distinctive attributes.

✕ **The ears:** Other than being positioned in the direction of the sound heard, the ears are usually a visible marker of inner emotion, be it fear (ears down pointing backward), confidence (neutral, facing forward), submission (down, to the side) or excitement (standing straight up, facing forward).

Long ears pose an extra challenge for animators. Indeed, at the part near the head, they react in a controlled manner, but from the middle part all the way to the end, they move involuntarily, like a thick piece of skin without any muscles of its own. All these motions will therefore come as a chain reaction from the rest of the body, and particularly from the base of the ears.

✕ **Antennae:** In nature, insect antennae do not react like ears at all. They are mainly sensory instruments used to analyze the surrounding environment or communicate with the other members of a group or species. However, in animation, we generally use them like mammal ears to express emotions. The reason is simple: humans are more accustomed to the non-verbal communication of mammals, and antennae are located more or less in the same place as ears.

TAKE NOTE!

When insects cast off their human traits for an action or a scene where they behave like an animal, they will show even more signs common to their species, such as using their antennae as sensory tools.

✕ **The tail:** The language of this body part is unique to each animal.

— Let's take a dog, for example: excitement will cause the tail to move from left to right very quickly, disappointment will cause the tail to lower, and submission (or fear) will cause the tail to curl under the dog along its belly.

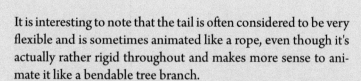

It is interesting to note that the tail is often considered to be very flexible and is sometimes animated like a rope, even though it's actually rather rigid throughout and makes more sense to animate it like a bendable tree branch.

— Cats are both a very familiar and very mysterious animal. A cat's tail is often animated in a very graceful, supple manner in which the motion's energy moves from the base of the tail up to the tip in fluid curves.

However, a cat's tail rarely makes big motions. The exception is if the cat is hunting: in fact, in this specific scenario, the tail swishes over the ground from side to side in a clear show of excitement.

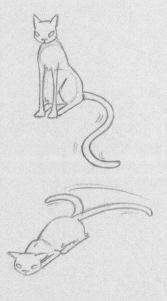

In most situations, though, whether having a rest or having a meal, the tail creates slight curves, which stay at the tip.

Nevertheless, in humanizing a cat (or any other animal with a long tail), we will take some liberties and give the tail a flexibility that we can use to our advantage. The fluidity of the curves will give the tail a snake-like quality and unconsciously convey to the viewer a notion of falseness, double-talk, slyness, or even manipulation. We can also use it in a similar way when working with a scenario involving seduction.

— A horse, like a cow or a giraffe, has a tail that hangs and moves back and forth in a very soft, flexible manner through almost its entire length. The most rigid part is located near the body, like with other mammals. In general, the tail isn't used very much except to swat away flies. It is rarely used to convey inner emotion, even if we observe some rigidity in case of stress (be it positive, like during a game, or negative, like during an attack), which is a natural follow-through from the overall tension in the rest of the body.

TIP!

When I animate a cat's tail, I like to use my hand and arm to act out the motions I think are right, which I film, analyze and, then, add to my character's tail. In certain scenarios, for example where we have seduction or slyness, my hand and arm motions will be exaggerated, but they will give me a good idea of whether they are accurate and timed right for the emotion I am trying to convey. Other times, my hand motions will be more discreet and human (for example, a hand slowly and softly tapping the armrest of an easy chair conveying a suppressed anger).

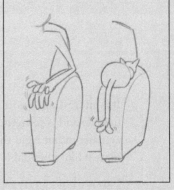

In non-verbal communication, instead we will opt for the image of an outstretched arm with the hand energetically waiving a handkerchief. We can act out and film these motions beforehand, and that way we can analyze how it will affect the rest of the scene and the overall timing.

— Other mammals, like cervids or rodents, use their tail as a signal of alarm by raising it up as high as possible and, sometimes, by revealing a contrasting mark on their skin, which will be easily noticed by the other members of the group. Do not hesitate to incorporate these details in your animations, even humanized ones, for a greater connection with the animal nature of your characters.

— For birds, the tail is a tool for steering, balancing and braking. Woodpeckers use it as a shock absorber during the very violent motions produced when pecking wood with their beak. In non-verbal communication, it is used especially in seduction and courtship. As for the eyes (eyespots) on the feathers of peacocks, these are a form of mimicry that peacocks use to intimidate potential predators.

All of these characteristics can be used in animation. Suddenly spreading wings can convey a sense of stress, fear, surprise (in a motion akin to raised eyebrows), but also anger, arrogance or aggressiveness.

> Don't forget that fluid tail motions can take the edge off a main animation that looks abrupt or jerky (see page 26).

When deployed slowly, a tail can convey an intent to seduce or manipulate, or even a degree of shyness.

— For fish, the tail (tail fin) is a tool of propulsion. We can also envisage it being used in an attack scenario, or, extrapolating further, in a vein similar to how birds use their tails, assuming the shape is appropriate. The animator is very dependent on the character's design when imagining other forms of expression using this appendage because, unlike bird tails, a fish's tail fin is vertical. Any time we use a fish tail, it's going to be perpendicular to the fish's face and eyes, particularly if our character is humanized.

In this way, non-verbal communication conveyed by facial expressions and attitudes is hard to combine with tail motions because the tail is hardly visible in most cases. On the other hand, if the fish's design is pretty similar to its natural design, with an eye on each side of the head, thereby preventing us from using asymmetry with the eyes,

the tail can be an enormous help.

—— Only certain primates and reptiles are fortunate enough to be able to use their tail like a hand to grasp objects (a prehensile tail). In animation, studios gladly have taken great liberties with this scientific fact and have attributed a prehensile tail to every kind of monkey, snake and lemur appearing in their films. In comedy, it is indeed very useful, and often very effective, to expand the prehensile functions of this "hand" to include human hand functions.

The "hand" at the end of the tail can even create a number of gestures behind the character that contrast with the initial sense conveyed by the character's speech or face, gestures that reveal its secret/hidden thoughts.

—— Lizards are well known for intentionally losing their tail when in danger (autotomy). This trait could be greatly exaggerated, for example, in a very frightened lizard that loses its tail whenever it feels the slightest emotion.

✕ The wings: These take the place of human hands quite naturally in animals that have them. They don't all have the same size or shape, but they transfer over pretty well. Not only that, we can also use the feathers as fingers.

The main advantage to wings lies in all the possibilities that their important size with respect to the body offers. Rather than looking at this particularity as a problem to be dealt with, look at it like an advantage: at any given moment, your character can hide behind its "hands" when its pathological shyness gets out of control; the intimidating effect produced by the spread wings turns a small aggression into a terrifying threat; a simple hand on the shoulder becomes a reassuring protection surrounding the second character's whole body; a big hand gesture becomes a lord's cape thrown across his body, putting an end to any discussion, etc.

✕ The fins: Fins are not as easy to use as wings. They are usually much smaller in proportion to the body and don't allow us to create the body language and gestures described above. In addition, it is very hard to use them to depict fingers. Instead, we ought to treat them like hands in mittens.

The specific design of your character can help you and expand your possibilities, but generally, the acting is mainly done by a fish's face and body motions

✕ Beaks: If you can transform your characters' beaks (the vast majority of beaks belong to birds) and you can modify their shape (regardless of which animation technique you are using: modeling clay, drawing, CGI), then you will have few constraints (compared to classic human mouths). It is nevertheless vital to take the beak's third dimension into consideration – a beak projecting forward – and to takes steps toward maintaining a harmonious design. Generally, the parts considered to be flexible are the corners of the mouth (located where the beak opens), the beak's lower jaw (equivalent to our lower jaw), and, to a lesser degree, the part on the upper jaw immediately over the open beak (equivalent to our upper lip which, being a beak, may need to undergo a slight transformation, for example, to form the Oo sound), depending on your camera angle.

TAKE NOTE!

The beak can open using a hinged or sliding system, or a blend of the two, depending on your design.

- Hinged system: the beak's jaws move apart with a rather open angle: the two tips of the jaws move apart, but the parts fixed to the face remain in contact with each other.

- Sliding system: the corners of the beak (in humans, the corners of the mouth) get longer and thinner to open the jaws and keep the lower jaw parallel with the upper jaw.

The beak's tip is usually the element that most quickly reveals a beak that is too flexible, if not regularly inspected at all three angles (facing forward, profile, overhead). Naturally, you can play the hyper-flexibility card if you and your team are in favor of it. But, if that's not the case, embellishing the facial expressions by modifying the tip of the beak may seem acceptable only so long as they remain rare and imperceptible to the viewer's eyes. We can help some extreme motions by delaying the beak, but if we do, it must be discreet enough to preserve the impression of rigidity.

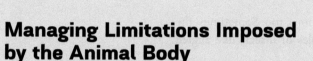

Managing Limitations Imposed by the Animal Body

With animals, sometimes certain body parts are added, but sometimes they disappear. For example, eyebrows can be absent from a character's design. However, in order to convey a complex acting, we have to compensate with some tail or ear motions, or by using clever timing and managing space carefully to emphasize body motions, as we saw with the faceless objects on page 188.

Comparison between human and snake body language for the same expression.

✕ We have seen that beaks can have their own limitations with respect to the human mouth, but we also know very well that the animal kingdom offers a plethora of different mouths we can use when we have to bring human qualities to a design or animation. We introduced the idea of harmonious design with the talking crocodile on page 103. Here, too, the rigid beak of a bird is going to pose a graphic challenge when changing from one extreme shape to another, for example, from an Ee or Ah sound to an Oo sound. We may be tempted to add or stretch the beak's shape artificially toward the tip, but the beak's volume doesn't appear or disappear from one mouth shape to another by magic. Shapes change, but the overall volume remains the same, and we must find the most harmonious solutions possible to transfer volume from one place to another. Here, the Oo sound that's going to close the beak on the sides must be offset by a narrowing of the upper and lower jaw. While this manipulation isn't very noticeable, this trick will help us out when it's time for lip syncing.

✕ The mouth of invertebrates has its limitations, too. Sometimes, the solution may be to animate the mandibles of insects like angled beaks.

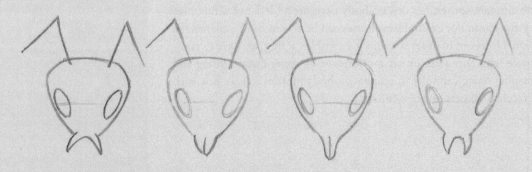

We can also invent humanoid mouths that don't exist in the real biological shape of these animals.

Finally, a last option can be to simply animate the body by squashing and stretching it to depict the chain reaction movements of a mouth we will never see but will clearly sense (this is particularly effective for mollusks).

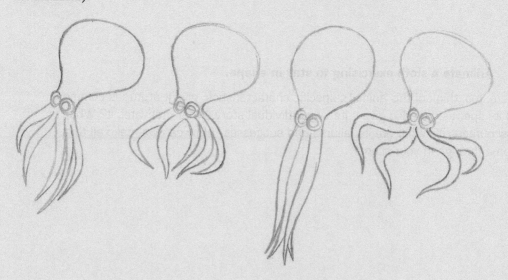

✕ Compensating with other body parts is one option, but we can also choose to use the mystery of an inexpressive face to create narrative tension and perhaps, later, a contrast that will generate a strong emotion in the viewer (laughs, tears, fear, etc.). One of the best examples is provided by a... human: the career of Buster Keaton, an actor and director of silent films in the 1920s, relies heavily on the unchanging stoicism of his face in the most extraordinary situations. To bring us back to animation, Droopy, the humanized dog created by Tex Avery, can be considered the drawn equivalent of Buster Keaton, in that his face has the same disappointed expression all throughout his adventures. The Roadrunner never honors his sworn enemy, Wile E. Coyote, with much emotion. He's content to sport the same half-mocking, half-condescending smile at all times, and to stand so tauntingly still before he sticks out his tongue, as if to punctuate the scene. A character with no facial expression can easily look intimidating, menacing even, but in some cases it may look rather mysterious, fascinating or cute if the soberness of its attitude recalls that of a melancholic child (like a *kodama* in the animated film *Princess Mononoke*). A total absence of expressivity can be enough to generate a sense of guilt when faced with a silently resigned being whose fate depends on someone else.

▶ **Animate a sloth exercising to stay in shape.**

Here, too, think of this animal's specific characteristics: give it attitudes common to its species, but also give it its own individual story. What motivates it? What discourages it? What are its failures and successes? How can we make all this come through in your scene?

NON-HUMANIZED ANIMALS

When animating non-humanized animals, a significant part of the work consists of careful observation and research. The logistics it takes to reproduce animals' characteristic motions forces the animator to look for references elsewhere. Online videos are invaluable. Nevertheless, we can also end up spending numerous hours hunting down a specific or a similar motion, but also a video that is clear enough, at an angle conducive to animation work, or with lighting showing enough detail.

Eadweard Muybridge's numerous series of photos will be a very a useful tool for jumping and motion cycles in animals. They are clear, and the angle, usually head on or profile, makes understanding the motion easy. The series includes a large number of animals. In addition, the individual photos are juxtaposed with a timing that is identical, or otherwise very close, to your animation timing. Lastly, the photos are arranged one after another and can be easily printed out and saved on your work table, or close to your monitoring screen.

Let us, now, look at a few specific aspects of animal morphology that would be helpful to know.

> **TIP!**
>
> Whatever your primary or local language, when doing your search, it may be very helpful to enter English terms in the search engine as well so that you get a wider range of results.

Wings and Flight

One species cannot impose its particular set of movements to all others in its entire order. Let's explore this idea with wings and flight.

✕ How birds fly and move their wings is all too often stereotyped and not given enough thought in the character being animated. Just as we find a wide variety of sizes and shapes in birds, we can also observe many different kinds of wing motions. However, when a bird is animated, its motions are often based on a crow's...

Yet, the sparrow and vulture, for example, don't move like that at all. A sparrow flaps its wings extremely fast. This very frenetic motion is often followed by a folding of the wings along its body when it momentarily descends downward.

We cannot consider this to be a gliding action, however, because a sparrow's wings are not extended to rest upon the air like many other birds, such as eagles or seagulls. The descent is not vertical, either, because of inertia (see pages 40-42), which continues to propel the body forward while gravity pulls it downward. After this period of controlled descent, as the inertia loses its force and gravity increasingly influences the downward motion, the sparrow flaps its wings again to resume its forward motion.

The massive wingspan of a bird such as the vulture means that its wings never move as fast as the wings of a small bird we might find in our gardens. Each flap displaces an enormous amount of air, and the bird's weight requires long wings to ensure it can remain in flight.

Many birds flap their wings a couple of times and, then, glide to continuing flying without losing energy, or they glide on an air current, like hang-gliders and paragliders do.

✕ When you establish the key positions of your flight, be sure to consider the body's weight and the animal's typical motion in the air: at what point during the wings' motion is the body going to drop slightly? And at what point is the thrust of the wings going to propel it upward again?

The wings create maximum resistance in the air when pushing downward by extending their wings as wide as possible, which propels the body upward. Then, as they move upward again, the wings fold in to generate as little resistance as possible in the air.

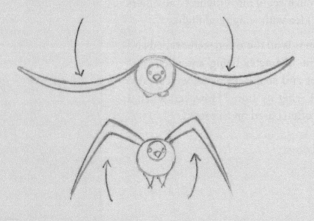

In fact, if they didn't fold in their wings, this resistance would cancel out the thrust and make the effort completely useless. Understanding the physics and the logic to motions is, therefore, absolutely essential in the field of animation.

What's more, the animator needs to ask: what are the body's inner motions, what reaction do the wings' cause on the pelvis, neck, head, and legs? What does the tail do and how does it function?

The way in which wing thrust affects body motions is most visible at the start, when birds take flight, since the inertia is still weak at that point and the body falls more with each flap of the wings. Birds anticipate this by squishing their body together. Additionally, the flight curve is not a smoothly ascending curve. Actually, birds "fall back down" every time the wings move upward, then ascend again every time the wings move downward, until they reach cruising speed, at which point these ups and downs become harder for the eye to see. The range of these upward/downward motions depends entirely on the bird's weight, of course.

EXERCISE

Animate:

▶ **a robin flying;**

▶ **a pigeon flying;**

▶ **an albatross flying.**

*Share your creations on social media with **#SecretsoftheAnimator***

✕ If we consider other flying animal species, we can observe an even greater variety of flights and motions in the air. Bats are not birds at all: they are mammals that have not followed the same biological evolution. Although their wings made of skin resemble birds' feathered wings, if we look at their skeletons, the differences are blatantly obvious.

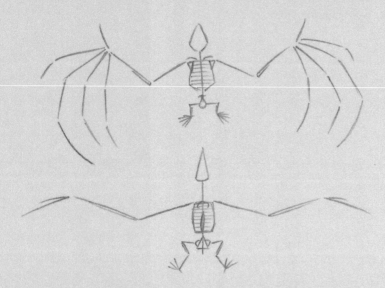

Birds don't really have fingers, but bats do, and their finger bones are much larger in proportion to their skeleton compared to humans and birds. Furthermore, the weight of a bat's body in relation to its wingspan and the weight of its wings is in clear contrast to birds. This affects its agility and what it can do in flight (a bat can turn totally upside down and hang from a ceiling seamlessly). There is also one other big difference we can observe: bats' wings are attached directly to their legs, which is not the case with birds.

In sum, it is imperative to carefully research the distinctive characteristics of the animals you plan to animate and diligently note the details that will make your animations more beautiful and accurate.

Jaws and Chewing

Just because humans and animals share certain elements does not mean they are animated in a similar manner. Indeed, these elements may not function at all in the same way.

As an animator, we can easily have the tendency to forget to check all the motions, including motions we can make ourselves... We have a jaw. Animals have a jaw. It would seem all you have to do is observe yourself chewing and apply your observations to your animation. However, herbivores do not at all chew in the same way as carnivores or omnivores. This very simple fact is, nonetheless, not quite well known. Shapewise, herbivores move their jaws from side to side and grind their food between their teeth. We can also observe this phenomenon when they yawn: a herbivore does not open its mouth in a fully vertical motion, as a human (or a cat) would; when it opens and closes its mouth, it has to move its jaw slightly to the side as it moves up or down.

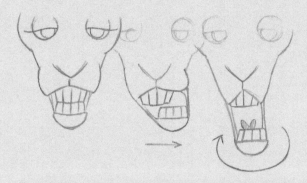

On the other hand, carnivores only move their jaw vertically, while the teeth cut up the food using a severing motion. When a piece of food gets stuck on a dog's teeth, it is very hard for the dog to remove it because it cannot slide it from its position with a side-to-side motion. It can only crush it into smaller and smaller bits between its teeth until the tongue and saliva make it disappear. Unfortunately, the out of control head movements the dog makes to dislodge the piece don't really help much.

Thus, the joint of a herbivore's jaw does not allow it to chew using the same motion as a carnivore, and vice-versa. By contrast, in omnivores the jaw joint allows both types of motion, and hence they can chew all kinds of food.

Thus, as humans, we may be easily tempted to animate jaw motions like ours. However, if we want our animations to be biologically accurate and in no way like humans, we have to research all of our character's body elements to make the details as realistic as possible.

Lizard and Bird Motions

The morphological differences in size (and mass) create big differences in locomotion.

Common to rocky, sunny environments all lizards move fairly quickly. For an animator, these motion curves hardly have inbetweens.

Similarly, a small bird makes frequent, short, abrupt, and sudden head motions. Its head turns a bit like human eyes, with little or no inbetweens and easing, depending on the distance traveled. And, just like with human eyes, a long distance (or a close-up) also means more easing.

Additionally, we observe that a small bird takes lots of minuscule steps from side to side. This stepping motion is very fast, with only one inbetween at the start, perhaps one inbetween in the middle of the step if the distance traveled by the body is significant, and a little cushioning at the end of the motion.

✕ The conclusion we can make regarding all these observations is that the smaller the body element is, the less inbetweens we will have. Of course, size is all relative. But, when we talk about size, we're talking more specifically about the mass moving from one point to another and size as it relates to how it's perceived by the human eye (the viewer's eye). As a general rule, when the mass in motion is small, the motions are smoother and, thus, quicker and faster, even if the muscle strength overall is also weaker. All things being equal, some species stand out from animals of a similar size or mass (like the cheetah or the flea). Here again, it is important to do good research before animating.

This same rule also applies to the human body: the eye moves very fast, with hardly any perceptible inbetweens. On the other hand, the legs are much slower, and their motion curves stand out more to the naked eye.

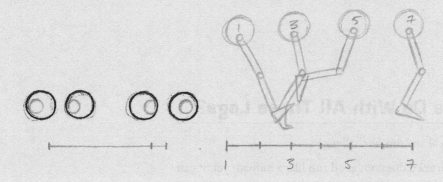

✕ This brings us to our second point: small sizes involve small distances or very fast speeds, and their animation curves do not stand out much to the eye. The animation curve of a pupil looking to the right looks like this in a wide shot:

Now, if we do an extreme close-up, or if the pupil in question is that of a giant, the curve will look like this:

A lizard in a wide shot moves according to this animation curve:

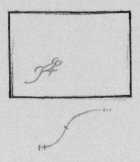

A giant lizard, or a close-up shot, will be like this:

What Do We Do With All These Legs?

This is both a technical and motor challenge.

✕ By nature, a quadruped does not at all run like a human; yet, it can totally be animated like a cartoon in a non-realistic, exaggerated way. Thus, we can simply animate it like so: we lift up the front legs and make them hover over the ground, then we raise the back legs into the air before all four feet touch the ground together.

A quadruped walking like in a cartoon can also look realistic, but here the poses are just as exaggerated as the timing: one foot up in each pose, for example.

Let's look at one last example using a cartoon style and a walking bird with very small feet and, thus, with no medial joints (the heel on a realistic skeleton). One of the legs lifts off the ground, raises up and reaches its maximum height, then descends in a forward motion before touching the ground.

✕ Realistic locomotion also depends on which species we are animating. Nevertheless, most common four-footed mammals move in a fashion similar to one of the following gaits:

— The walk is a four-beat gait: the feet are in contact with the ground at four distinct moments. The hind leg lifts up first and takes the place of the front leg on the same side. The shifting motion on the right side is just ending when the front right leg touches the ground as the left hind leg lifts up for the shifting motion on the left side.

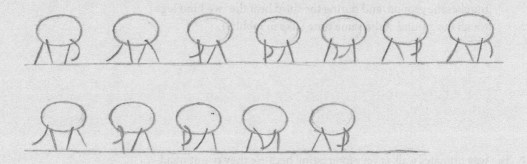

— The trot is a two-beat diagonal gait. The front left and hind right legs move at the same time, then touch the ground. Next, the front right and hind left legs move.

Some animals have a trotting gait on the same side, like the camel, whose front and hind legs lift on the same side and touch the ground together, before the legs on the opposite side do the same thing.

—— The canter, i.e. Canterbury gallop, is a three-beat gait, and a full gallop is a high speed, four-beat gait in which the four legs touch the ground one after another. In a canter, the leg the furthest forward touches the ground, and the animal uses this leg to propel itself forward off the ground. We can observe two different canters.

In the first, during the second beat the hind opposite leg touches the ground, and during the third beat the two remaining legs (diagonally across from each other) touch the ground together (like in horses).

In the other canter, during the second beat the second front leg touches the ground, and during the third beat the two hind legs touch the ground at the same time (like in rabbits).

× The way primates walk is very interesting because they're not quadrupeds; they're bipeds. However, the way they walk on two feet is rather peculiar because they frequently lean on their upper limbs (particularly when walking).

Thus, the baboon has an almost completely diagonal gait (like a horse's trot), except that there is a two frame shift where the front hand touches the ground slightly after the hind diagonal leg. The joints are loose and relaxed, the motion is rather slow. We also observe a pause before the opposite hind diagonal leg lifts up for the next cycle.

The tail hangs in a semi-controlled fashion and sways from side to side. Baboons tend to jump in a rather erect, rigid manner, even from side to side; the whole body moves at once, and the limbs are practically straight.

✕ The way birds walk is usually fashioned after "big" birds. Small birds actually move by hopping on both legs, which are slightly out of sync.

For their part, crows often walk according to the following sequence: they lift a leg off the ground and move it right above where they are going to put it down. Then they put the leg down. Next, the body gradually leans on the leg it has just put down. It only leans on the leg on the other side once it is firmly on the ground (while cushioning the sudden shift).

✕ Insects have even more legs, typically six, which doesn't make an animator's job any easier. Ants, for example, have a four-beat gait (two beats for a three-leg sequence, then two beats for the other three legs). A front leg and a diagonal middle leg move at the same time (first beat), and about halfway through this motion, the hind leg on the same side as the front leg in motion lifts up (second beat). For a brief moment we can see all six feet touching the ground right before the cycle begins again on the other side.

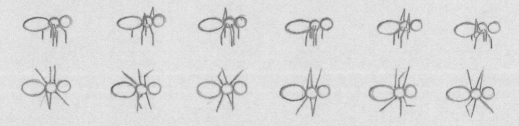

This whole time, the body moves forward in a straight line, albeit in a rather awkward, not so stable manner.

✕ Spiders (as well as scorpions, ticks, and other mites) have eight legs, which distinguish them from insects. Nevertheless, despite the increased number of legs, the walking cycle is ultimately easier than with insects: it's simply two identical beats (one beat per four legs). If we assign a number to each leg from front to back and use the letters L for left and R for right, the cycle is as follows: L1, L3, R2 and R4 move first (first beat), then R1, R3, L2 and L4 move next (second beat).

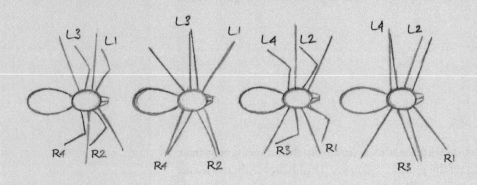

I would like to finish this book with a little story that I think is important to keep in mind as an animator, or as a creative in general.

Keith Jarrett is a very well known American pianist, particularly in the world of jazz. The year was 1975. Keith was on tour in Europe and about to play a concert one evening. It was a prestigious venue. He was already well known and widely recognized. However, when he was showed the piano he was supposed to play at the concert that night, it was a disaster! It wasn't tuned, certain keys didn't work at all, and others had to be depressed with an incredible amount of force. He asked for a replacement piano. It wasn't possible. Consequently, he refused to play under the circumstances and attempted to cancel the concert. The concert organizer was young, and it was her first big show of this kind. She begged him to play in spite of the circumstances: her job and career were on the line. He accepted reluctantly. The curtain opened. Throughout the performance, Keith Jarrett struggled mightily with the piano, sweating blood and tears. At times he had to stand up to be able to depress the uncooperative keys hard enough, and his groans could be heard throughout the concert hall. He had to improvise and play a totally different program from what he had planned because of the missing notes on the piano. The circumstances forced him to be creative, to find solutions, and to use all his know-how and sensitivity to give his audience a quality performance. Somehow or another, he made it through the concert. When he finished, he went backstage, embarrassed of his performance. But, in actuality, the audience had been transported... The moans, the body movements, the sweat: it was all proof of an artist intensely living through his art. *The Köln Concert*, as it is known today, is Keith Jarrett's most famous and widely recognized concert.

I take away two lessons from this story...

1. We don't lay the blame on the instruments or the working conditions. We have to be creative, resourceful. We must be ready to produce quality animations no matter the factors, the design, the technique, etc. Ultimately, we emerge smarter and more skilled.

2. We can really struggle and hit a ton of snags during a shoot, and we can think it's the worst animation project ever, but the viewer will never know how hard it was to film. The viewer has no preconception, no context. The viewer only sees the final product. And the final product can be quite extraordinary! This may be precisely because you have to draw on all of your knowledge, your instinct, and your sensitivity for the final product to have such an impact. Don't judge your work too hard without, first, getting some outside feedback; instead, congratulate yourself on successfully making a quality product, thanks to all the little things that make up your talent and make you unique.

We have talked a lot about what happens on screen because this is clearly the most important consideration. Now, it's time to go over the conditions necessary for your work.

× Take note of the instructions you are given. There may be a lot of them: instructions from the director about the acting and the action, but occasionally technical instructions to animate a camera movement, a special lighting effect, the appearance/disappearance of an element mid-shot, etc. This will help you not forget anything, particularly when the shoot takes several days.

Moreover, this little habit gives everyone confidence. Plus, one must always look out for their reputation. Animation is not a big industry. Take care of what image you wish to project.

× Make an efficient shooting schedule. Shoot any shots with elements in common at the same time (e.g. the scenery, specific lighting, animated elements, etc.). This way, you will reduce transition times.

× Divide the work up, delegate tasks. Specializing in one task without worrying about what others are doing creates reflexes that allow you to work more efficiently and, consequently, more quickly.

× When shooting right in front of a camera, wear black or dark matte colors. The color of your clothes can actually reflect light into your scene and cause issues. If you are wearing light-colored clothes, talk with your director of photography to see if you need to change or stand in a particular spot during any shots. Also make sure you don't cast a shadow on the scene or create a reflection on a small window on the set (or another glass surface).

× Pay attention to how outside light can affect your work. Make the set completely dark and make outside light appear/disappear intelligently (dark curtains, paneled doors, etc.)

× Make sure everything is glued and fixed in place, and make sure everything on the set and in the area of movement is tied town. From the first frame to the last nothing must move. Any movement will be captured by the camera and will create a mistake (a "hitch"). Consider securing your camera (tighten all the set and adjustment screws, glue the tripod to the ground, and protect the area around the camera to prevent any accidents), secure the set to the animation stage, and the stage to the ground. Do not use Gaffer's tape or Blu Tak®. They are flexible and are, therefore, unsuitable for properly securing your items. Use hot glue. It hardens as soon as it dries and is, therefore, more suitable. It can also be removed with lighter fluid and leaves no residue when applied to non-porous surfaces (plastic tables, concrete floors, etc.)

× Empty and clean up the space. Do not store anything else on the film set. Create work spaces off to the side of it.

× Think about your rigs and where to place them so that the post-production team responsible for removing them in post has to do as little work as possible. Moreover, it is always helpful to talk to your colleagues about what they specialize in so that you can get an idea of what they do and, thus, make their job easier.

✕ When choosing techniques, do not forget about time constraints. If a chosen technique requires deformations and transformations (often, modeling clay), you have hours of work in store. Is it warranted, conceptually and graphically?

✕ Think about how to preserve your materials over time and, occasionally, in conditions of extreme heat. Everyday modeling clay dries very quickly; therefore, try to find good quality clay. As for organic foods (vegetables, fruits, meats, etc.), they obviously change very quickly.

✕ Before you start animating

— Mimic and act out the scene.

— Time or analyze how long your actions will take.

— Draw the main poses on an exposure sheet.

— As you prepare, choose what your big moments will be and surround them with neutral/small moments to make them stand out.

✕ While animating

— Place some marks on the screen (and the set too, if the marks are off camera) to make sure your curves are consistent.

— Always be checking your animation curves by looking at your three, four, or five preceding frames (or more, if necessary, there is no other fast and steady rule except aiming for the best quality). Calmly check each point on the element's animation curve frame by frame, up to the very last frame. You will have to do this numerous times, forward and backward, until you have checked all the points on all the curves of all the animated elements. In straight-ahead animation, if we only look at the previous frame without going back any further, we have no idea what direction the curve is moving in or the timing gap between the two poses.

— Pay attention to your cushioning and rebounds when a motion comes to a stop. It is rare to slow down too much, especially when you are getting started, and it is easier to take it out than to add it later.

— Think about desynchronization, and energy transfer/shift: where does the motion start and where does it end? Which elements move in response to others? How does the transfer of energy affect each element? And how does the timing affect it?

— Desynchronize your big actions, too, so that they all don't happen in the exact same way.

— Act out the motion or have it acted out to establish the actions, to check how credible the character is, and to test out different options, but also to determine what affects the other parts of the body.

— Not everything has to move all the time! Arrange for some pauses in the animation when possible and when necessary. You'll make the animation clearer and easier to read for the viewer.

— Think in terms of real time: 24 frames, that's only one second! Six frames, that's only one quarter of a second!

— Don't be lazy. Do what needs being done. Sometimes you have to go back, start over, make a new mouth, resculpt an element, remove too much of something, something that doesn't look good, something showing a gap or letting light in, etc. Keep in mind that the best animations have been worked on by animators who have paid attention to every last detail.

— Physically step back from your work at regular intervals. From time to time, stand a few meters from your screen and watch your animation from a distance, especially if it is intended for television or computer screens.

— To catch potential errors, watch your animation in a classic mirror, or in a virtual mirror (symmetry function) available on your image capture software. The animation will look unrecognizable, and this way you will be more likely to see any mistakes, imbalances, or wrong/unreadable motions.

— Be careful about animator's blindness. You know what is going to happen, so everything you do will seem easy to analyze to you, but a new viewer does not know what to expect, and their reaction time will not be at all the same as yours. Regularly ask people who are unfamiliar with your project to give you their opinion, and make sure to get their impression of how they understood the action (without giving them any clues ahead of time, that goes without saying).

— Animation requires concentration because there are so many things to manage at the same time. You cannot get inside your colleagues' heads, you do not know when an animator is in the middle of calculating or planning a complex motion. Do not bother your collaborators, and make it so they don't bother you while you are working, either. Take breaks off set, and respect other people's work and concentration on set.

— When you are animating, retain the memory of the gesture, the tactile memory of the direction and the spacing of each manipulation. You will save precious time and more easily prevent errors in your animation curves. Take a break when you are passed that movement; finish it before you get distracted or interrupted.

— Try making an "animation route" that is identical for each frame: animate all your elements one after another in the same order, without stopping, so that you don't forget any.

— When you animate cycles, try to find tricks to help you animate faster and to avoid checking where you are at every frame. Sometimes, I give a name to each pose of the cycle, for example for a run cycle: passing, up, contact, down; sometimes, I draw arrows on some adhesive tape I stick off camera as close as possible to the element, e.g. for some shakes (left 1, left 2, left 3, right 1, right 2, right 3). This doesn't mean I don't have to check the animation curves, but this makes manipulation quicker and reduces the number of trips back and forth from the monitoring screen.

✕ Method and organization are very important, just like accuracy, meticulousness, attention to detail, patience, perfectionism, and mostly a sense of observation and analysis. These qualities are essential in an animator and can be acquired at anytime with determination and hard work.

Enjoy yourself! Have fun! Be creative! Anything is possible in animation.

Animation is an entirely artificial art. The lighting is done in total darkness, the scenery and puppets are made from raw materials, and the life we bring to our characters is depicted in unique frames, one pose after another. Everything is thought out, calculated, planned and executed with an intent and an objective. The objective is the viewer, their thoughts, their understanding of the work, and the feelings it will generate in them. It is important to know a few rules applicable to all viewers that influence their relationship with your film and, hence, your own relationship to your creation..

× The viewer always looks at the element that is acting, talking or moving the most, if not for the entire duration of the action, at least when there is a change of pace.

× When we want to draw the viewer's attention to an important element, we avoid distracting the viewer with elements moving around it at the same moment.

× The viewer always looks at the character's eyes. Other actions are mostly perceived by peripheral vision. The viewer can certainly cast a few glances to read the action of another element on the character or elsewhere in the picture, but the viewer's look will return to the eyes of the character in action once the action has been analyzed and is stable.

× If the character in action looks at another character or element in the picture, the viewer will, presumably, follow suit and also look in that direction. This is a very effective way of moving the viewer's attention to where we want at the right moment.

× The viewer instinctively looks at the second character when the first finishes talking; the viewer only comes back to the first character if it starts talking again.

× The viewer may take a moment to look at the surrounding environment and the other characters if the main action is obvious or easy to follow without directly looking at it.

× Laughter is a result of a contrast, a surprise, a sudden unexpected change in the pacing. For example, a character racing at full speed around a curve suddenly crashes into a mountain. The unexpectedness of the situation, the surprise and the shock will trigger laughter first. Secondly, the laughter will also be fueled by the fact that human beings have a tendency to laugh at the misfortunes and minor catastrophes they witness when they know they aren't real or serious. The same logic applies to emotions (for example, when a character, who has thus far been very calm, suddenly bursts with anger).

× In the same way that we need to give the characters time to react, we also need to give the viewer time to read the action and the image. Naturally, the viewer needs time to focus their attention. We mustn't begin any meaningful action while their attention is still focused on the previous shot or while they are still analyzing actions that have just occured.

Therefore, think about:

—— how much time your character needs to think;

—— how much time the viewer needs to analyze the action;

—— how much time the viewer needs to internalize the action (time to generate a feeling of empathy).

× If the subject appears on screen in an extreme close-up shot (a close-up of the face, for example), the viewer will look at the subject's eyes. The mouth, on the other hand, will be at the edge of the frame and will be harder for the viewer to read. Thus, the mouth's motions will need to be bigger and less subtle, or significant enough to draw the viewer's attention.

× Pay attention to the camera angle and the actions' timing. If one element is far from another on set but they still look close in two dimensions on screen, do not animate actions that could be misinterpreted by the viewer. In fact, this could give the impression that there is a real interaction between the two elements (for example, a hand reaching in the direction of a second element, and the second element moving at the same time). Actions must, therefore, be separated by a pause.

× Two points of interest to bear in mind:

—— It takes longer for the brain to analyze/recognize a face than to read/recognize a written word;

—— The brain is always looking for connections between the elements/information it receives (and it usually finds them).

× The secret to the connection between the viewer and your characters (humans, animals, objects or creatures of all kinds) is empathy. And to create empathy, the viewer needs to relate to your characters or recognize the humanity in them. Animating your characters in a human way isn't necessarily a must; we may actually want to leave some distance between the viewer and certain characters. But if we want the viewer to be transported by the story, to feel that they are a part of our hero's adventure, we need to animate them according to human body language.

× **Animation Curve:** A graphic representation of a motion's speed (spacing between poses) and direction (the curve's geometric shape), there being one curve per each mobile element (or for each individual part of a given mobile element). This curve can totally be a straight line. When we refer to an animation curve, we don't give any indication about its direction, shape or angle.

× **Exposure Sheet:** A work document that can be adapted according to necessary information. On an exposure sheet, we usually find the project name and shot number, a column with the numbers of all the frames of the shot, one column for each character, the phonemes to be posed for the sound of each frame, and even directions for specific actions, special effects, lighting, etc.

× **Lip Sync:** The action of synchronizing the mouth's movements with the dialogue, syllable for syllable and sound for sound.

× **Rig:** An external support used to immobilize an animated element. With a rig, not only does the element not move during the capture, it also makes it hard for it to deviate from its animation curve when handled. A rig can be invisible or visible (if visible, it will have to be removed using computer software); a rig can tie an element down or suspend it in the air (this allows elements to be held in the air or in an unbalanced position).

× **Hitch:** A mistake in an animation curve giving the impression that the motion has gone off its smooth curve, i.e. that there is a glitch.

× **Time Lapse:** A filming technique consisting of framing a real-life scene (such as a landscape, a street, a whole film set, etc.) and taking pictures at regularly timed intervals. The sequence of images is then played at 24 frames per second, creating an effect that speeds up and compresses time.

Concepts to Distinguish

× **Straight-ahead animation (i.e. "frame by frame") *vs.* key-frame animation.**

—— Straight-ahead animation requires the animator to animate elements frame by frame in chronological order, starting with image 1, then 2, then 3, etc. up to the very last frame without leaving anything out along the way.

—— Key-frame animation requires the animator to determine the first and last pose of each animation curve (key frames) and then "fill in" the rest of each curve, between the key frames, with "inbetweens" that stay within the animation curve.

× **Animation films *vs.* live-action**

—— Animation films are films in which each motion of each element is crafted frame by frame.

— Live-action films consist of scenes with living beings and objects moving according to the laws of physics. These films are shot at real speed.

✕ Pose *vs.* frame

— A pose is the result of manipulating an element and putting it into a fixed position to appear in a frame. There can be several frames for a given pose.

— A frame is a picture of a scene taken by a camera. The frame is a unique photo of the scene. We can shoot several frames in a row without altering the scene to change a pose.

✕ "On ones" vs. "on twos"

— We animate "on ones" when we animate one pose per frame. This is also known as "animating at 24 frames per second."

— We animate "on twos" when we animate a pose that we shoot twice in a row, in other words when we create two distinct pictures (which will be shown one after another) for one pose of the motion. This is also known as "animating at 12 frames per second."

✕ Shot *vs.* scene

— A shot is defined by the starting and stopping of the camera: we start the camera on a new shot, and, at the end of the shot, we stop the camera. Most of the time, what usually causes a change in shot is a change of scenery or a change in camera angle.

— A scene is a concept that is way less technical than a shot. We group together a few shots into a scene when the shots have characteristics in common, such as a particular moment in the story ("treasure is discovered") or a certain scenery ("conversation in the hallway") before there is a change.

Page 18 exercise

A bowling ball falls and rolls.   A star transforms into a circle.

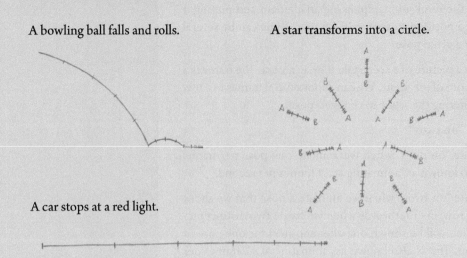

A car stops at a red light.

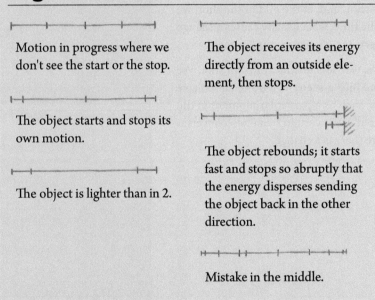

Page 22 exercise

Motion in progress where we don't see the start or the stop.

The object receives its energy directly from an outside element, then stops.

The object starts and stops its own motion.

The object rebounds; it starts fast and stops so abruptly that the energy disperses sending the object back in the other direction.

The object is lighter than in 2.

Mistake in the middle.

Page 37 Exercises

Exercise 1: The two toes in question are the main animation, where the energy originates from. The other toes move very slightly too (the closer ones move more, and the farther ones move less); they comprise the secondary animation. The legs and the rest of the body make up our tertiary animation; their motions are even more subtle.

Exercise 2: Here, we will naturally want to put the main animation on the arms and face, since they are the most emblematic body parts of this gesture. However, this is precisely what we mustn't do. Where does the energy for the animated motion come from? What is the source? Here, it is the chest that suddenly fills up with air. Our secondary animations (the follow-through from the chest filling up with air) will be visible in the shoulders, the hips and the body tilting in space. In the end, the face and the arms will only be tertiary animations, even if they are the most visible. For their part, the hands will be a couple of "bonus" animations, i.e. the cherry on top of one entire beautiful animation.

Page 46 Exercises

Exercise 1: The body lifts up as the left hand pulls out a sheet of paper. The character looks at it, then the body hunches over while the head turns toward another sheet of paper in the cardboard box. While the left hand tosses the sheet of paper, the right hand plunges into the box to grab another. Next, the body hunches over further and the left hand returns. The body lifts up again as the right hand raises a sheet of paper, then the left hand plunges in again as the right hand tosses the sheet of paper, and so on.

Exercise 2: As the character is gathering the water, it is looking where to empty the bucket. When the character lifts up the bucket, it looks back at the water it is bailing out, but its hands are still in the process of tossing the bucket water overboard.

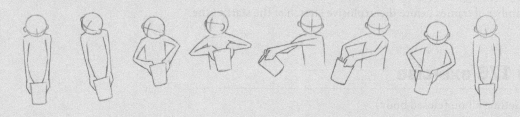

Page 56 exercise

For a cartoon, the main difference is that we have to add a clear anticipation in which we scrunch the face, squash the head into the shoulders, and scrunch the body over approximately four to six frames (depending on how intense we want it to be) and, then, explosively stretch the whole body and face into a long, exaggerated expression of surprise very similar to the illustration shown at the top of page 53. Naturally, we will remember the cushioning when coming out of the explosive motion. Note that we can also make the head shake during the squashing in the anticipation. In this case, this anticipation will likely require more frames than the explosive stretching.

Page 77 exercise

To start, we have a elastic band under extreme tension, as reflected by a tensely shaking hand. The character is concentrated, the face scrunched toward the eye aiming at the target, the head tucked into the tense shoulders. We allow this elastic tension time to build up. In turn, this will increase the narrative tension in the scene. Next, the character lets the elastic band go, which loosens and explosively launches the stone (in a blur and in a straight line toward off camera). Thereafter, what we see is a sequence of body animations in response to the action, according to the chain of priorities (energy transfer, rebounds and cushioning). It's a type of recoil, typical of a gunshot for example. In this case, the recoil will be less extreme because the object isn't as heavy, and the energy transfered is less. After this, we have a neutral moment where the character analyzes the situation. We continue animating the character – it has to remain lively – but here the animations need to be subtle, almost imperceptible, to create a contrast with what came before and what comes after. When the character causes damage, we animate an anticipation of surprise that we squash for a few frames (four to six) and, then, explosively stretch and very subtly ease on the rebound (or return) after the most stretched pose. After this comes an expression of surprise and fear that the character has to hold for at least a second. We must also animate this second very subtly, so as to bring the reaction to an end in a contrasting fashion. Next, the character runs away. We start this with an anticipation in the opposite direction of the main motion (think of cartoons like Tex Avery, Chuck Jones, and any others showing a wide variety anticipations like this) and follow it with a burst of motion blur over one or more frames toward off screen, depending on the desired speed (don't forget that the faster the character runs away, the more noticeable the anticipation needs to be, not just physically in terms of how exaggerated the squashing is, but also in terms of time, in the number of frames before the explosive stretch at the start of the run).

Page 176 exercise

—— Getting hit on (closed body)
—— Boredom
—— Shyness
—— Concentration

ACKNOWLEDGMENTS

This book was written in 2016-2017 while I was working full time on several productions one after another. It goes without saying that I would never have been able to complete it without the actual help of several colleagues. My long-time friend and extremely talented animator, Julianna Cox, helped me immensely by graciously agreeing to draw additional illustrations for this book. She also provided constant support throughout the writing process.

I would also sincerely like to thank my very talented colleague, Christophe Peladan, for carefully proofreading the manuscript from his perspective as an experienced animator. He was the first person to give me enthusiastic feedback about the content and usefulness of this book, thus rescuing me from the spiral of doubt in which every author, I am certain, finds themselves sucked into during the long months spent alone writing.

I would like to thank my colleague, and director of photography, Nathan Sale, for his assistance with the photographic illustrations. The materials and knowledge he provided were critical to helping me finish this titanic task in record time.

The idea for this work was not entirely my own. The idea came from my many colleagues and friends who, seeing my professional notebook, encouraged me to share the knowledge I had acquired from the many productions I had worked on over the years. I would like to give special thanks to Gareth Owen, who convinced me that this book would be of interest to aspiring animators.

I would also like to sincerely thank Céline Remechido and Christelle Doyelle at Pyramyd, who opened their doors to me to hear my proposal. They put their trust in me and showed me their unwavering support throughout the writing process. This book wouldn't exist without their precious guidance and availability, or without the contributions of the graphic designer, Philippe Brulin, who made it look absolutely amazing.

The original notebook this book is based upon contains many notes about techniques I discovered by trial and error, after mistakes, or simply after thorough reflection; however, a good number of the tips and tricks were shared directly by my fellow animators, directors, modelers, set designers, directors of photography, and camera operators at all the studios I've had to opportunity to collaborate with. I would like to especially thank my colleagues at Aardman Animations, in Bristol, for generously sharing their knowledge in the interest of quality animation. I would particularly like to mention Dave Osmand, who unfortunately left us in July 2017. He was my first mentor in the profession and the most generous and most insightful of all. I would also particularly like to mention Terry Brain, as well, who left us in 2016. He was one of the most enthusiastic, most effusive animator-directors I've ever known, and he was a constant inspiration to the young animator I was back then.

I also wish to thank two directors who always succeed at creating a collaborative working environment where equality is valued (a precious thing in our work): Jeff Newitt and Richard Webber. The former, in addition to his qualities as a director, created and animated one of the films that inspired me to become an animator. The latter is like that good friend you meet up with on Wednesdays to play with the chemistry set and conduct experiments all afternoon. It is always a tremendous pleasure to animate on his projects; he shares all of his ideas and gives me an enormous amount of freedom, which allows me to push the modeling clay to its creative limits.

Lastly, these acknowledgments would not be complete without a few personal thank-yous: to my brother, Mathias, who gave me the idea of becoming an animator in 1994 after seeing how obsessed I was with animation shorts, and also to Cwyn Solvi, who encouraged, supported, and reassured me tirelessly throughout the entire writing, illustration and publishing process.

This books belongs to you all, and I sincerely hope it makes you proud.

THE AUTHOR

Julia Peguet is a professional animator who has worked in animation since 2000.

After getting her start in drawing, she transitioned to stop motion and clay animation, which has always been her true passion. In 2004, she joined the team at Aardman Animations (creators of *Wallace and Gromit* and *Shaun the Sheep*), a studio with which she collaborates to this day. She also provides animation for other studios in France and abroad from production to production. She has had the remarkable opportunity to animate characters for *Wallace and Gromit*, *Shaun the Sheep*, *Creature Comforts* and *Pirates*, but she has been fortunate to work on other productions, such as the Sony Bravia's Play-Doh commercial, with its multi-colored rabbits.

In recent years, she has also taught animation master classes and workshops for film and visual arts programs, in addition to teaching professional training courses for adults.

9780367252007